W9-AMA-712

Tropical
Interiors

Contemporary Style in the Philippines

by Elizabeth V. Reyes
Photography by A. Chester Ong
Styling by Aida Concepcion

PERIPLUS

Published by Periplus Editions (HK) Ltd

Copyright © 2002 Periplus Editions (HK) Ltd

All rights reserved. No part of this publication
may be reproduced, stored in a retrieval
system or transmitted in any form or by any
means, electronic, mechanical, photocopying,
recording or otherwise without prior permission
of the publisher.

LCC Card No. 2002107863
ISBN 0-7946-0019-0
Printed in Singapore
Book design: mind, London

Additional styling credits: Ivy Almario (pp12–17);
Leo Almeria (pp122–127, 142–145); Albert
Avellana (pp32–39); Connie Castro (pp86–91);
Roland Laurena (pp18–23); Budji Layug
(pp24–31), Yola Perez-Johnson (pp82–85);
Eric Paras (pp108–115); Impy Pilapil (pp32–39);
Johnny Ramirez (pp92–97); Wendy Regalado
(pp54–59) Ernest Santiago (pp60–65); and Chito
Vijandre (pp116–121).

Distributed by:
North America, Latin America & Europe
Tuttle Publishing, 364 Innovation Drive,
North Clarendon, VT 05759-9436, USA
Tel (802) 773 8930; Fax (802) 773 6993
Email: info@tuttlepublishing.com

Asia Pacific
Berkeley Books Pte Ltd, 130 Joo Seng Road,
#06-01, Singapore 368357
Tel (65) 6280 3320; Fax (65) 6280 6290
Email: inquiries@periplus.com.sg

Japan
Tuttle Publishing, Yaekari Building, 3F,
5-4-12, Osaki, Shinagawa-Ku,
Tokyo 141-0032, Japan
Tel (03) 5437 0171; Fax (03) 5437 0755
Email: tuttle-sales@gol.com

Cover: Modern entrance to the home of Jaime
Augusto and Lizzie Zobel; furnished with giant
abaca loveseat by Delfin Penero; floor lamp
by Val Padilla, sphere vase by Carlo Tanseco,
Princessa piña shawl from Palawan. Cover
styling by Aida Concepcion.

Back cover: (clockwise from top): Nature setting by
Dita Sandico-Ong; vine-inlaid desk set by Louisa
Robinson; laminated display plate from Bacolod,
Negros; and Gerico Austria's atrium *sala* by Eric Paras.

Page 1: Fiery orange draperies made of *abaca* and
rayon, by fabric designer Elisa Reyes of Bulacan.

Page 2: An artful setting in the Jose Quiros home,
by Ivy Almario; painting by Bernard Pacquing.
This page: Modernist accent vases hand-wrought
in stainless steel, by Markus Schmidt for Firma Inc.
Opposite page: Contemporary glass trays and
serving dishes by Bobby Castillo; functional art
displayed at the Avellana Gallery.

Contents

New Tropical Design
Soulful Creativity and 'Philippine Moderne'

A new generation of Filipino designers has, in recent years, been making design waves outside the Philippine archipelago. Designers are combining metal technology and native rattan weaving; splitting, bleaching and using *abaca*-rope in stylish ways; laminating coconut shells and twigs into biomorphic artworks; making soigné lounging chairs from seagrass and organic lamps from handmade paper; mixing fibreglass pipes with twigs and shells—and soulful creativity.

In September 1999 , a designer consortium called "Movement 8" made a big splash in the furniture exposition in Valencia, Spain, displaying unique home items not yet seen on local shores. Curator Budji Layug had selected a stylish array of clean-lined, geometric furnishings made by Filipino designers—realizing his own vision of a purely *moderne* sensibility (deriving from Art-Deco, Bauhaus, and natural materials). The show stunned viewers, turned heads and opened doors. After Valencia, "Movement 8" won acclaim at virtually all the major furniture expositions, including New York's prestigious International Contemporary Furniture Fair in May 2001—when the Filipino designers took home the top award for craftsmanship.

In July 2001, the *Washington Post* carried the exciting design news that was syndicated across the USA—the Philippines' largest market for furniture.

Opposite: The Quiros condo's abundance is showcased with Zen-like balance. Chinese traditional furnishing is synchronized with Asian modern art: a gauzy painting by Romulo Olazo; modern Japanese print by Toko Shinoda; and the living room's pivotal oil, "Neurotic Zen Master", by Lao Lianben. The bamboo vases and violet organza cushions are from Kish, Makati. Balanced design by Ivy Almario and Associates.

Above: Three *capiz* and resin finger bowls, by Shell Arts Company of Cavite, upon Japanese inspired bamboo veneered tray, designed by PJ Aranador for Rebena Co. of Bacolod.

Left: : At the FAME 2001 exhibition, designer Josef Crisanto taught the values of modularity, versatility, flexibility—and colourful whimsy—in small living spaces. His special setting brought new manufacturers to the fore: Vienna Furniture Inc. created smart modular seats that can be realigned for different needs; the rose-lamp and three frames comprise wood shavings art by Papuri Crafts; the stuffed pillow and tall coco-bead lamp are by Catalina's Embroideries of Cebu.

Opposite: The FAME show's Best Display booth, showing new products by Padua International, presents the statuesque Gia lamp in beached Philippine mahogany with her wide cylindrical shade flaunting a faux-*capiz* finish. Fine leather armchairs are complemented by black wood accents featuring a hand carved, indented treatment inspired by Ifugao artefacts. Designs by Val Padilla for Padua International.

Style writer Patricia Dane Rogers spread the word: "Filipino designers are using the wealth of traditional, indigenous materials they always have—volcanic rock and forest vines to coconut palm wood and narra wood—but the young experimenters are using them in decidedly non-traditional ways. Natural materials are being beaten, pressed, polished, woven and stained to make urbane, up-scale, high-end furniture in innovative and modernist designs." Said Christopher Reiter, owner of a Washington DC furniture boutique. "This stuff really rocks! Within the trade, everyone knows that furniture makers in the Philippines have moved up the value chain. They're on the fast track; they have leapt ahead of other Asian manufacturers."

The main draw-card of the New York show was the *Pigalle* armchair. This curvy topiary form, composed of wiry steel bound in *abaca* twine, was created by 31-year-old Kenneth Cobonpue from

Cebu, Philippines. Cobonpue epitomizes the new aesthetic. He had previously designed an award-winning Yin & Yang armchair, a cubist wire framework wrapped in open-weave rattan. "I wanted a feeling of lightness and transparency, but to achieve it using natural materials," Cobonpue explained. "We're all designers who share the same belief in the mixture of a modern sensibility and an Asian sensitivity to craftsmanship and natural materials."

The modern-thinking Movement 8 was nurtured by two design gurus: Ms Araceli Pinto-Mansor, executive director of the Center for International Trade Expositions and Missions (CITEM), a semi-governmental body promoting Filipino products; and curator Budji Layug, one of the country's most successful interior designers. They invited ten designers to contribute to the image-raising effort and expose their work to a global market—with unprecedented success.

Right: The folkloric sofa, Laso (Loop), is a mixed-media design featuring flattened bamboo, leather, mat-weave, and whole rattan vines, bent to demonstrate the extreme flexibility of the material; by Ramon Castellanos, Disegno en Asia (Cebu).

Comments Mansor: "We're starting to create sophisticated designs for the modern world! Although the Philippines offers neither high technology, nor formal training or government support to boost the furniture industry with more global exposure and focused efforts like these, design-consciousness is being raised—and will filter down to the rest of the industry." Mansor calls the main characteristic of Philippine designs a soulful creativity. "Filipinos have innate talent and creativity with natural materials—but up to now, our products have been too ethnic," she says. "We have to uplift our whole image for the sophisticated global market."

Earning international recognition has been a slow process and a constant dream long nurtured by Budji Layug. His design-driven circle of Movement 8 produced new furnishings embodying a common sensibility: clean, contemporary lines, very *moderne* profiles (between Art Deco and Bauhaus), and sleek geometric forms with the natural feel of indigenous materials. Presenting new items of wood, glass, stainless steel, leather,

bamboo, *abaca*-hemp and rattan, Layug imbues each Movement 8 setting with a light, resort-like feel, but an unmistakable aura of sophistication. "Many items follow a stylish modernity that harks back to the '50s but with a more refined feel."

The prime achievement of Movement 8 has been: elevating the Philippine image and a design-driven consciousness within the industry. Having Filipino-made furnishings recognized for their creative and innovative designs in the highly competitive (i.e. price-driven) Asian market.

Industry pioneer Nicholaas de Lange muses on Filipinos and their talent for design: "They are quick to absorb trends. They are not just manufacturers, but generally have an appreciation of style from living with varied colonial masters." Filipinos have the ability to 'make do' with perennially limited resources—this has naturally bred the talent for creativity which is the cornerstone of the Philippine industry today. When the supply of one particular material was diminishing, they moved to mixing materials … and the world was gifted with a new, relaxed yet stylish look. Style watcher Elsa Klensch named it "Asian Fusion".

Not long ago, the country was merely a source of raw materials. From a middling cottage industry 20 years ago, the vital design sector has emerged, putting the Philippines firmly on the map with its furniture, decorative products and household accessories. Two Philippine institutions played big roles in the organic evolution of crafts and design: The Design Center and CITEM. The Design Center, created in 1973 and directed by modern artist Arturo Luz, was the first body to focus research, development and experiment upon humble native materials. Its mission was to design aesthetic products for the country's nascent crafts industry. Hands-on graduates of Luz Design Center include Val Padilla, Dem Bitantes, Joel Enriquez, Jun Delingon, Olive Loyola—all seasoned designers today.

From 1984 , it was CITEM—led by Mina Gabor, trade show ringleader—that fomented a dramatic crafts revolution. Seeing native handicrafts stagnating, Gabor pulled Philippine woodcraft and basketry out of the doldrums and led the way into the export world. She recognized talent, rallied local designers, and stimulated both design and markets. Foreign consultants were contracted to train, expose, and teach local suppliers "to satisfy the overseas markets".

"Mina had vision, drive and brazen enthusiasm," says Chito Vijandre, the eclectic interior designer. "She had both gut-feel and vision. She took our tourist crafts out of the mould of long-necked wooden heads and Miss Universe chairs. She had foresight, challenged designers, upgraded skills, then flogged our stuff to the world!" Gabor stimulated small-time provincial cottage industries to go urban. She implemented exhibitions in the country and overseas. Under her gaze, the Philippines metamorphed itself from supplier of raw materials and low-cost manufacturer to a creative innovator of hand-crafted décor. Cebu, in particular, developed her small furniture trade into a major industry, turning out fanciful mixed-media products. These creative designs garnered, for the whole Philippine industry, the moniker "the Milan of Asia".

In the '80s Filipino architects and designers earned individual successes. In 1987, Ched Berenguer-Topacio's "Petal Collection" of wrought

Above: Graceful 'cutgrass' resin accents by Louisa Robinson reach up to a multi-framed paper-art composite by Tess Pasola of Mindmasters Inc. Filipinos' new crafts designs have blithely crossed the line towards organic artistry.

Left: Ifugao Suite setting: black and gold bowl and matching mug are "vintage Lanelle Abueva" stoneware, on modern serving tray in black fossil stone and glass, by Leo Almeria.

iron and leather furniture was awarded the highly coveted Roscoe Award. About the same time, rustic-chic bamboo furniture by Budji Layug was selling to Bloomingdales, USA. Layug became a brand-name designer for his graceful, well proportioned furnishings—especially his signature products which used bamboo and rattan. The Philippines gained a foothold as an innovative supplier of classy tropical furnishings, while Layug shone as the doyen of an organic *moderne* style.

Philippine furniture and crafts have, according to designer Chito Vijandre, reached another creative level in the new millennium. "Filipino designers are not trendsetters nor originators, but creative innovators. Best at handmade, handcrafted products, we have a real ingenuity with natural materials —what high-tech machines cannot do! Very interesting things are happening now. One company harnesses ethnic *abaca-tnalak* cloth and adds coco-bead trim—for the most chic pillows in town. In Davao new designers like Ann Pamintuan have been able to create something so very modern

Right: Consultant Crisanto lends a fresh designer touch to a casual dining table at the FAME show. The half-back chairs are by Vienna Furniture, the seat pillows by Catalina Embroideries. The sunny crockery is by Cardinal Ceramics.

Opposite, left: The wiry oval seat by Davao-based Ann Pamintuan of The Gilded Expressions is an edgy sculpture that has won accolades in the West.

Opposite, right: Fused metal wire as tealight ball by Ann Pamintuan.

out of rustic methods and basic materials. Her creations of metal wire, welded and fused like a net, are so individual and edgy, so far from mass-produced!" Unusual items are coming out of Negros in the form of throwaway materials which are used to make modern designs.

Thus the Filipino forte for innovative crafts in natural materials and high-end modernist furniture has high-dived into the 21st century. Designer Leo Yao experiments with bleached banana trunk and twisted raffia for giant armchairs. Modernist Milo Naval designs bold, modular furnishings wrapped in earthy natural materials—and confident attitude. Val Padilla creates eclectic furniture in fine leathers, handmade paper or seagrass. Ed Yrezabal produces golden Permacane furniture using a high-tech lamination process on rattan—for items that lend a graceful presence to resorts and lanais. And who knows what Cebu's rising star Kenneth Cobonpue will design next, after his airy cubist seat and curvy topiary *chaise*?

The Filipinos' designer niche has been cast,

aiming to lead the industry beyond the competitive marketplace. Budji Layug is backing it wholeheartedly. He wants passionately to embrace the culture, arts and crafts, and unique materials of the whole region and create a truly "Asean style". As he sees it: "Our only edge is innovative design for the high-end market. There's no choice: to survive among competitors with more technology, cheaper labor and more materials, we have to design cutting-edge products for design-driven clients—and stay several steps ahead of the copy-cycle!"

Tropical Interiors celebrates Philippine interior design by exploring the most popular styles—the Elegant, Natural, Urban and Eclectic. But the more exciting matter vibrating between the pages is the Philippine *moderne* sensibility evident among the homes and décor products. This new style book is indeed more about Filipinos' soulful creativity—the invention, experimentation and individuality of designs that swim ahead of the rest.

Overleaf: Moroccan gazebo in the garden. The Zobels' processional black-and-white curtains have been reinvented as an exotic Moroccan tent within a glass-enclosed garden pavilion. In the corners hang Spanish wrought-iron lantern-lamps. Hand-plaited designer *abaca* rug, ottoman and side table are from Soumak, Makati. The dainty Dalmatian model is Pongo.

Tropical Elegance

Contemporary Asia shines through this elegant Philippine style that merges traditional artefacts with modern crafts. Designers employ subdued textures, fine Philippine artwork, and masterly forms of furnishings.

Previous page, bottom row, middle: Lindy Locsin hallway with Val Padilla floor lamp.

Left: The mat-upholstered Millie Love Seat by Yrezabal bears a graceful demeanour, backed by the S-curved Molina screen. The organic divider—a wood and steel grid filled in with a natural vine mesh—along with the Alberto table lamp, were designed by Val Padilla for Locsin International. The golden chair with a knotted armrest is the Malena Lounge chair by Yrezabal. The ecru silk and hemp rope 'carpet' is an exotic fabric creation by Silk Cocoon.

Contemporary Cane

Natural light and myriad shades of white are mandatory design elements for smart contemporary homes in the Philippines. In their Makati house, Gregg and Aida Marshall have personalized these basics by adding creamy Javanese sandstone, linen-white fabrics, filmy *katsa* muslins and a conscious use of the tropical light to form an elegant home.

After some eight changes of address in 12 years, Indonesian-born Aida Arifien Marshall has gleaned an appreciation of the comforts inherent in American design and successfully married these with the traditions of Southeast Asia—in this case, a fine collection of the Asian crafts she so loves. She viewed some 90 Makati houses before deciding on this big, white house for the family's new residence.

To extend the house's views and afford more natural light, Aida revamped the central areas by installing sliding doors and a large picture window in the *sala*. Their walls, and the *lanai* floors, were refurbished with creamy sandstone tiles imported from Aida's Javanese hometown, Jogyakarta. Teakwood furniture and sandstone jars—part of the Arifien family's business—decorate the interiors. A white-upholstered sofa folds around a massive, square coffeetable, remodelled from an antique bed. Seated in this elegant Asian *sala*, everyone gazes out toward a picturesque Balinese water garden, designed by Aida's mother.

Below: The statuesque Gia lamp with a *capiz* finished shade; Julio woven black-leather chair; and Metro, a three-level light table, are contemporary chic designs from Padua, Yrezabal and Locsin. Decor bowls and flower vases wrapped in black twine and wooden vessels with woven rims are modern accents by Carlo Tanseco for The Store.

Right: A window seat with Oriental airs. The well stuffed Nobu Accent chair (by Yrezabal) has won apt recognition in the Japanese market. Nobu sits by Dumbo, a barrel-shaped light table (by Locsin). The modern setting is complemented with ceramics by Rivera Clay, Makati.

It is on the Marshalls' airy *lanai*, which looks like an open-air stage with drapey white curtains—that our stylist Aida Concepcion assembles an array of fabulous, contemporary Filipino furnishings. Playing against backgrounds of natural sandstone, *katsa* curtains and garden greenery, she orchestrates several romantic-contemporary settings.

The furniture items of this spread are produced by leading Philippine designers for the overseas market. The matted loveseat, Millie, and three stylish armchairs are manufactured by the Yrezabal Corp, local inventor of the arty but exclusive Permacane process. Permacane is an high-tech method of laminating rattan cane to form sculptured limbs for creative furniture.

There are other remarkable designs in a tropical-modern mode. The Molina screen is a graceful confection of *nito* vine applied in a 'crazy weave' format hiding its unique S-curved steel frame. This see-through screen and the two modern accent tables, Metro and Dombo, each with translucent side walls, were created by furniture designer Val Padilla, for exporter Locsin International. The oil-polished Relax *chaise*, made with handwoven *solihiya* (open cane-weave), comes from Lightworks, naturopath designers of "organic furniture that flows with the cosmos".

Above: Languid scene in Madame Arifien's Balinese garden. A long lounging *chaise* by E. Murio Inc. combines fine Malacca cane and exquisite colonial taste. Two stone accent balls made of Pinatubo volcanic lahar are from Amazing Space, Shangrila Mall. The colourful *malong* cloth is from Zamboanga, courtesy of stylist Aida Concepcion.

Right: The languid Relax *chaise* combines plantation mahogany and *solihiya* (open cane-weave). This modernized planter's chair and the *runo*-grass tray on the floor are examples of eco-friendly, organic furniture design by Ravi Singh of Lightworks, Manila. Two oversized candle stands entwined in rattan vine and a hollow rattan globe are designs by Carlo Tanseco for The Store Inc., Makati. The stoneware tea set is from Regalong Pambahay, Ortigas.

Opposite, clockwise from top left: Tropical accessories. The organic stoneware pieces are by Ugu Bigyan (artist potter of Quezon Province), while the vine tray is by Mr Renato Vidal, designer owner of First Binhi Corp, décor-product suppliers with sheer genius for recycling nature's vines and grasses. The nailed-down wooden vase and the stringey, twined vase (picture directly below) are designed by Carlo Tanseco for the Store Inc. Tanseco trained in architecture, but jumped right into designing crafts for his Gen-X lifestyle store. Three colourful resin lamps are retro-modern designs from The Raphael Legacy of Cebu; the resin-mosaic lamps won the Mugna Award 2001 for their seventies-mod design. They stand upon an unusual copper-finished table with three legs, from Lightworks, Manila. A Philippine shell suite by the window: translucent *capiz* shell stars in two diamond-cut lamps; while egg shells provide a natural crackled finish on a white sphere vase; designs by Carlo Tanseco for The Store Inc., Makati. White linen throwpillows, courtesy of Aida Marshall. The most naturally elegant flatware in town are made of the unique mother of pearl shell, finely detailed with hand wrought silver and black *kamagong* wood; designs by Cosonsa of Cebu.

Hacienda Romance

This hacienda-style home with a distinct Mexican flair was the first residence designed by the young Andy Locsin, a Harvard-educated, progressive architect. Inspired by the modern works of renowned Mexican architect, Luis Barragan, Locsin designed a large homestead for the Spanish-Filipino, Jaime Augusto Zobel and his Colombian wife, Lizzie. An elegant home, it was conceived to evolve continually in style as their family grows.

There's already been a fiery new incarnation to the house. The modern, all-white stucco walls have been rekindled in a Beijing terracotta red tone and many of the *lanai* rooms have taken a dramatic turn—towards an unabashed romantic flavour not previously there. Lizzie Zobel derives her many inspirations from mixed international sources, then collaborates the arrangement with her favourite designer, Yola Perez Johnson, owner of the *abaca* carpet shop, Soumak.

Yola Johnson has a gift for mixing rustic materials and romantic imagery. She entered the field of interior design through the manufacture and export of Soumak's *abaca*-hemp carpets, hand-woven pieces much sought after by clubs and resorts (today every rustic-chic residence has one or two). Johnson wields her talent for home-decor using the most native, natural materials and then imbues her creations with pizzazz within its interior setting. She in turn credits her savvy client for being "so open" to her exotic, exuberant ways with home design. She draws attention to the Zobels' giant padded coffeetable (see right), created from wrapping a woven mat around a massive wooden

Opposite: The Zobels' casually elegant *lanai*, dressed with romantic Oriental overtones. Here is the indoor-outdoor lifestyle at its best—with a picturesque view of the bamboo grove. The fanciful candlelight chandelier is by Yola Johnson.

Left: The classic Philippine *butaka*—an elegant *kamagong* wood version of the traditional plantation chair (made by Kit Roxas of Tawalisi)—stands regally alone on the open air *lanai* amid a processional colonnade. A fine, patrician *piña* scarf hangs over its arm.

Below: The other corner of the *lanai* is occupied by large wicker sofas, palm fronds and white muslin curtains. Grounding the space is a black Chinese wedding cabinet and an imposing central coffeetable, wrapped in fine *banig* or matting. Still there's room for a rustic lampshade of natural *nito* vine.

Overleaf: The refreshing Asian tropical breakfast table. Gathered around a long solid wood table (from Tawalisi, Makati), eight finely finished cane armchairs with Chinoiserie flavours were designed by Yola Perez-Johnson and produced by E. Murio. Natural cane furniture balances well with the airy *paminggalan*, a traditional Filipino kitchen cabinet with slatted wood panels.

Above: The lime green dining room is a romantic contemporary suite composed around two six-seater modern tables made of dark *supa* iron-wood, said to be three centuries old; two modern Chinoiserie lantern lamps from Italy; a French carpet; and the Victorian-style impressionist painting of "Juan Luna's wife" by young artist Mariano Cheng.

Right: A once-nondescript corner-space was transformed into Lizzie's "sexy bordello" room. The orange sitting room is now a dramatic conversation piece, draped with layers of curtains and furnished with stuffed Victorian sofas, mixed Chinese furniture, and glowing cylindrical lanterns made from a delicately torn piece of antique damask silk.

box, and praises Lizzie Zobel's acumen by commenting that "most homeowners could not work with those big proportions". She also custom designs furniture such as the romantic loveseat, a Victorian-style two-seater wicker sofa with a lacy, almost transparent, backrest and unusual pointed, onion feet. "It's a very romantic loveseat," she smiles.

The owner and the designer share a love of candle-lit chandeliers, hot tropical colours and voluminous drapery. They're proud of their Moroccan-style tent, a glass-lined *cabana* in the garden, separated from the house and the deep blue pool.

Lizzie's smart black and white curtains formerly in the lanai have been recycled as tent-style drapery—a perfect foil for the Zobels' Dalmatian.

Johnson is proudest of the orange bordello sitting room, a dramatic space draped at all doorways with shimmering *abaca*-rayon curtains, created by fabric designer Elisa Reyes. Inside, one wallows in stuffed sofas covered in silks, satins and fantasy. Warm light glows from several rectangular Chinese-inspired hanging lamps, designed around a piece of antique damask silk Lizzie Zobel brought back from her travels.

Opposite: The "La Sagrada Familia" is a rare and precious religious icon, here enthroned over a Philippine *divan* with Napoleonic curved ends and fine bone inlay.

Above: The guestroom's regal bedstead. The headboard is an ornate wooden panel, fully carved on a rose theme. The lush metallic-threaded curtains, held back by two pivoting bedside lamps styled by Yola Johnson, are from Silk Cocoon, Manila.

Left: The country-elegant look reposes on Florante Aguila's spacious *lanai*. The contemporary wicker sofa chairs by Mehitabel of Cebu are complemented by organic accents from designer Renato Vidal of First Binhi Corp—two leafy towers and a shaggy fruit basket, large *nito* vine planters (left rear), and wild golden grasses on the coffeetable.

Country Elegance

Filipinos have evolved a local architectural style known as Philippine Mediterranean. Traits of the Italianate villa-by-the-sea have migrated to the tropics: Filipino architects have imported red-tile roofs, white stucco walls and spacious *salas* flowing out to airy *lanais*. Interior mezzanines overlook the sala while small balconies decorate the second floor. Below, arched doorways and warm-coloured tile floors create wide spaces for entertaining, tropical Manila style.

Florante Aguila's Mediterranean-style house in Makati is significant as the last residence designed by national artist and architect, Leandro Locsin. The cantilevered *porte-cochère* at the end of the long driveway gives the house a certain Locsin ambience as do the wide interior spaces adorned with giant antique furnishings from old churches and houses. The *sala*, dining room and TV-den are furnished with elegant wood pieces, supplied mainly by Designs Ligna Inc., a company evolving from traditional to more contemporary lines. The classic Philippine wood items are combined with a stunning array of Chinese furniture, heirlooms sourced around Asia.

The Filipino rustic style blends well with this Mediterranean-style abode when applied to the *lanai*. This shady verandah is open to garden views, and outfitted with the most comfortable, informal, rustic furnishings. Interpreted by urban homeowners this means country colours, elegant wicker furniture and a touch of nature in the accessories. The rustic contemporary *lanai* of the Aguila abode—here styled by contractor Connie Castro—showcases wicker furniture from Cebu's leading manufacturer,

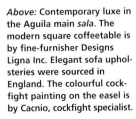

Above: Contemporary luxe in the Aguila main *sala*. The modern square coffeetable is by fine-furnisher Designs Ligna Inc. Elegant sofa upholsteries were sourced in England. The colourful cockfight painting on the easel is by Cacnio, cockfight specialist.

Top right: The inner den speaks quietly tropical and tastefully refined in the classic conventions of Mehitabel furniture (Cebu). The floral painting is by surrealist-modernist Onib Olmedo in an unusually happy period.

Mehitabel, alongside modern designs by Manila-based companies.

Contemporary ideas in rustic furniture include biomorphic lounging chairs and standing lamps fashioned from handmade paper. These are designed by Val Padilla for Locsin International, a leading furniture exporter who has successfully tapped into the Italian and German markets. Created from twisted seagrass woven over steel tube frames, the singular Penelope chair and the two-part lounging chair, Angelo, are ideal for any contemporary space. The two upright, faux-Japanese paper lamps, were conceived originally for the Italian market: "The Italians wanted lamps that reminded them of the Orient," recalls Padilla.

Stylist Castro uses the *lanai* too to showcase earthy yet chic accessories made of stoneware and creative grasses. Quezon potter, Ugu Bigyan, displays his latest organic creations along with a giant black stoneware rock, meant to imbue an urban home with rustic flair. And displayed on every tabletop are the varied, ultra-organic, grass arts by Renato Vidal of First Binhi Co.

Left: Aguila's antique *kamagong mesa altar* is dressed with thoroughly modern accessories as the indigo blue stoneware jars and a painted plate by potter Ugu Bigyan of Quezon. The giant laminated mirror with a 'wood-strings parquet' motif comes from Johanna Lacson, the recycled crafts' designer of Bacolod and Manila.

Left: Rustic modern furnishings in all-natural materials. Penelope is a sculptural seagrass seat conjured from the plump grass plaited over a steel tube framework; it's comfy too. The shapely paper lamp makes a modern statement for Filipino design as oriental, organic and ornamental. Both designs are by Val Padilla for Locsin International. Accent cubes bundled in natural twine, by Renato Vidal for First Binhi Corp.

Right: Angelo, a stunning two-piece *chaise*, is composed of twisted seagrass woven over steel tubing. Comfy lounging is guaranteed in this contemporary and cursive design by Val Padilla for Locsin International, Manila. The orange *tnalak-abaca* pillow is from Tadeco, Davao, while the ethnic weaving from Special Things, Makati.

Right: The springtime
pavilion. Modern treasures
and antiques sit in perfect
harmony in the informal
lanai. The contemporary sofa
set in woven seagrass (by
Primafil) straddles a Chinese
square coffeetable of bamboo
and cane. The darkwood
table with five drawers and
bone inlay is a rare *mesa
altar* from Batangas. The
carved drum on the left is
from Java. Silver and wood
accents comprise folk artefacts and modern handicrafts
arrayed together.

Asian Refinement

Fernando Zobel's Manila house is an icon of contemporary Asian elegance. It exudes all the funda-
mentals: refinement of taste, simplified luxury and
a distinction that comes naturally, thanks to the
owners' cosmopolitan breeding. There is a polished
discipline in the Zobel credo: invest in quality either
antique or modern, display objects you love, and
highlight rooms with fine Filipino art. And, enlist the
expertise of professional designers.

The Zobels' first investment was the choice of
modernists Andy Locsin and Ed Ledesma for the
sleek architecture they call Asian Fusion—a synthesis
of Thai, Japanese and Javanese lines. Their second
decision was to commission designer Johnny Ramirez
to coordinate the interiors. Ramirez's seasoned
hand integrates old and new, harmonizing traditional
and modern accents, and fashions a timeless
elegance evident in the subdued modern surfaces,
subtly varied textures, and in the masterly forms
of new furnishings which seamlessly unite the traditional and contemporary.

Zobel's collection of Filipino antiques was, from
the start, planned into the design of the three-
pavilion house. Ramirez integrated these by custom
designing new pieces to complement the established forms. Filipino heirlooms such as *mesa altar*
(altar tables) and inlaid *bauls* (trunks) take genuine
pride of place as functional furniture. Every room
is accented with artwork by modernists such as

Right: The formal *sala* with serene olive distinctions. Johnny Ramirez designed this subdued setting around a slatted darkwood coffeetable in the *gallinera* style by wood artist Omeng Osmundo. An ottoman stands on native wooden tops as feet. The feathery touches of green are Catherine's choice of papyrus. The calligraphic painting is by modernist Lao Lianben.

Far right, top: The interim hallway between pavilions is marked with a procession of antique musical instruments from Mindanao, some of Fernando Zobel's favourite Philippine artefacts.

Far right, bottom: Johnny Ramirez's modern guest's washroom features fine natural textured wallpapers, a large mirror wall, a slab of black stone as counter and a transparent glass bowl serving as the sink.

Above: The oriental dining room is spare and elegant, expressed in olive hues. The table comprises clear glass over carved stone pedestals. Chairs are dressed in linen, accented with shell tassels. At the head of the table, a metal art sculpture consecrates the meal and the diners as they break bread.

Left and below: The master's bedroom is the essence of refined simplicity, while being comfortably appointed with art objects and heritage furnishing. Ramirez designed this long freestanding head-board 'island' to hold drawers on one side (see below), and the 'floating' bed platform on the other, seen at left. Two large wardrobes—a dark *kamagong* antique aparador and a two-toned solid wood TV cabinet—are both unique heritage items that grace the Zobels' casually elegant lifestyle. The exquisite ivory heads and silver-tipped *salakot* (chieftain's head-gear) are—very aptly—the head honcho's own personal collection.

Right: The modern writing desk, the *escritoryo*, is a graceful orchestration of fine Malacca cane and black matting, by E. Murio. White tiger lilies are Catherine Zobel's personal touch.

Below: A cozy corner of the formal *sala*, designed round a simple modern coffeetable by Omeng Osmundo; an elaborately inlaid wooden chest; and an exquisite oil portrait of Catherine Zobel by romantic modernist painter Romulo Galicano.

Zobel (Fernando's uncle), Lao Lianben and Bencab, while an exquisite painting of Zobel's wife, Catherine, hangs in the formal *sala*—work of master portraitist, Romulo Galicano.

The *lanai* is an eclectic showcase for rattan-wicker sofas and wood furniture enhanced by tropical colours. It includes Zobel's remarkable Asian collection: a Tausog ritual drum from Zamboanga, traditional Javanese dining chairs, solid wood stands made from old sugar cane grinders, antique *santos* figures and silver-tipped *salakots* (hats). Rare Buddhist statuary is poised atop even rarer *mesa altar* tables from Batangas while *kamagong* wood *butakas* (planters' chairs) mix with contemporary armchairs by Ralph Lauren and a matching, cush-ioned sofa by Primafil.

Ramirez proudly brings tribal craftsmanship into the guestroom through padded headboards covered with earthy red *t'nalak* cloth, a tribal weave from Mindanao. The master bedroom features a 'floating' bed raised on its low platform, and a two-toned, bookend *kamagong* TV cabinet, both designed by Ramirez and made by masterjoiners, Osmundo. The Ramirez-designed cane-weave headboard is a two-sided piece with cabinets on the reverse executed by E. Murio, sophisticated caneworkers. All around are a series of fine ivory heads—treasures of the refined honcho, Fernando Zobel.

Above: The dramatic red
guest room. Red walls, red
curtains and a black *abaca*
lampshade counter balance a
baroque style bone-inlaid
cabinet from Batangas. Tall
twin headboards, covered
with modern *abaca*-hemp
weave, were designed
by Ramirez to show off the
hand-loomed craft of Davao.

Tropical Flair

This chapter presents an elemental style that delights in Nature—air, water, plants—and in the use of natural materials—wood, clay, natural fibres, stone, and bamboo. When worked into interior designs, the outcome is settings that are romantic, sensual yet practical—and tropical.

Previous page: Chimes, buoys, bamboo chair, and stone head by Ernest Santiago. Open walkway by Benji Reyes. Vigan jars by Belen King.

Left: In King's bamboo meditation alcove by Rod Cornejo, the nature masterpiece in red vine and bamboo is re-styled with white silk drapes and covers by Silk Cocoon. The blue cushions are from The Store, Inc., Makati, and the sky blue wood-shavings screen is by Papuri Crafts of Quezon City.

Holistic Living

Organic style indicates the predominant use of natural materials as well as arts and crafts with a natural form. On a higher plane, organic refers to a holistic or humanist philosophy within a natural home. Organic space lets in light, is in tune with nature, and lifts one's spirits with its wholesome vibrations.

This 10-year-old Makati house is an open-plan residence of rambling, free flowing spaces, as elegantly rustic as a holistic home could be. It's owned by Belen King, holistic thinker, matron of the arts, meditator, and avatar of Brahma Kumaris' alternative lifestyle. Amid the conventions of her neighborhood, she has simplified her life to the natural, essential and aesthetically rustic. The magnificent garden and lower-level *lanai* areas were the work of the late Rod Cornejo. The contemporary living and dining rooms are by interior designer Yoyoy La'O.

Cornejo's nature-textured art still thrives indoors and out. Ms King's office is a raised mezzanine on wide polished wood floors with a long, sliced wooden trunk defining the open-sided space and bearing Cornejo's signature red-vine weaving in its corners. Ground level floors are solid, earthy and paved with giant slabs of *piedra* china (ballast stone) and an expanse of greenish-slate stone. Ceilings and beams show off the finest Filipino hardwoods: yellow and red *narra*, and *kamagong*. The owner's inner sanctum is an all-bamboo meditation room, with natural light, open air and handcrafted vine screens—a thoroughly organic design conceptualized by Cornejo.

Below: By the brick wall—black leather chair (Padua); black-shade lamp on a wood cone stand (Renditions; Alabang); candleholder by Carlo Tanseco (The Store Inc.); and stoneware vases (Rivera Clay, Makati).

Right: The Permacane Pavilion, an elegant *lanai* setting with roughhewn Mactan stone walls, displaying graceful permacane furniture pieces; a standing floor lamp with embrossed acrylic shade by Padua; biomorphic resin art accents by Cielito, Cebu; and a garden scene painting by Jose Trinidad of Vancouver. The Madame X half-moon sofa and coffeetable, with the sinuous Natasha chair on *pointes,* make a *soigne* statement.

Within this rustic chic framework, stylist Aida Concepcion assembles an eclectic array of contemporary furniture and accessories. In the central *lanai* setting against roughly-hewn Mactan stone walls are several sleek, upholstered armchairs from Yrezabal, made with the distinctive Permacane. The Madame X half-moon sofa and coffeetable make a contemporary chic statement matched by Natasha, an armchair with sinuous golden legs branching out from its tan leather seat like dancers' legs on *pointes*. The graceful forms by Yrezabal are complemented by a dark wood floor lamp by Padua, outstanding biomorphic table accents by Cielito and a garden scene oil painting by Jose Trinidad.

The pool deck and courtyards are ideal settings for modern furniture. Two award winning classic-modern designs by Ched Berengeur-Topacio take pride of place: the Petal lounge chair, which won a Roscoe Award in 1987 and the handsome black Matador, made of carabao hide and hand-beaten wrought iron. In a cozy red-brick corner sits the signature La Padua, a tailored, black leather armchair, designed by Val Padilla for Padua International.

Left: This floor setting by stylist Aida involves a wood-shavings standing lamp (Papuri Crafts); copper-and-silk runner (Silk Cocoon, Makati); *abaca* throwpillows (Amazing Space, Shangrila Plaza); and other accessories.

Above: Bamboo rusticana settees amid the garden stones. This rare collection of bamboo armchairs and sofa was handmade by the finest master craftsman of Vigan, Ilocos Sur, Ms King's hometown. The red and black fabric runners are traditional hand-weavings from the Tingguian peoples.

Right, top: Traditional elements in a modern arrangement. A finely inlaid *baul* (wooden trunk) from Muslim Mindanao is installed next to an antique *santo* (Catholic saint figure). Both of these are displayed upon a solid bench of Philippine hardwood, propped upon an old sugarcane grinder hub.

Right, bottom: Gracing the holistic home are Mrs King's array of statues and saints: an antique ship's bell for announcing visitors' entry; a cherub carved on the wooden posts; a wooden friar in robes, welcoming all pilgrims.

Right: Tropical architecture ideas realized in Benji Reyes's rustic Asian-fusion house in Antipolo. The main pavilion contains an open-air *sala* clad in dark *ara-al* stone and runo grass from the Cordillera. All furnishings are his own woody artworks, designed and created from recycled hardwoods.

Below: Linking the levels stepping down the hillside are wooden decks and bridgeways as this one (accented by a paper lamp by Wendy Regalado). Beneath trickle several interconnected water ponds for families of carp.

Rustic Individualist

"He bends it against its will. He whips it into shape. It obeys, it dances, it undulates."—Writer Rachel Medina best captured furniture designer Benji Reyes's unique way with wood. "There is a clean aesthetic to his furniture, but it retains a sculptural, fluid look and feel. The play of texture is part of the appeal." Recently Benji Reyes has also become an inspired architect, applying his talents for recycled wood into building a three-pavilion Asian house, terraced onto a hill-slope of Antipolo, and presiding over four rippling ponds.

Benji Reyes's romance with wood started in 1982, when he had emerged from university as a sculptor eager to work with wood. Reyes decided to apply his creative talent to make 'functional sculptures', wooden artworks that would be passed on as heirlooms. He used only second-hand lumber and cast-offs, gathered mostly from demolished houses. For two years he was apprenticed to a master cabinet-maker and perfected a handcrafted method, bending, shaping, fitting and rubbing the recycled wood according to his visions. He emerged a furniture craftsman "who puts his soul into every single chair".

Carina, his jazz-singer wife, became the marketing manager and priced the works high, standing

Below: Soft-touch stoneware coffee pot and cups by Lanelle Abueva (Benji Reyes's Antipolo neighbour); cookie bowl made of laminated coco-shell, by Al Carona of TN International; and square food cover made of old *piña* and bamboo twigs by Wendy Regalado.

Right: The guests' washroom is a earthy corner with mango-hued walls. A huge wooden slab becomes a counter to hold a stoneware sink by Lanelle Abueva. Deep indigo tiles serve for watery splashbacks, and bright tribal fabrics for accents.

stubbornly on principle: "This is an artwork not just a piece of furniture!" They refused to bend to the whims of clients' tastes. Benji chose the artist's path, went the long mile alone, stayed away from mainstream politics and became known as the *ermitaño* (hermit) of Antipolo.

"It is a crafts workshop for six workers not a business for manufacture," continues Carina. "He works with six cabinet makers, who have no one single specialty, but can make all his standard pieces. It's a very exacting process, manually engineering the old wood into new modern works." It took 12 years of chair-making before Benji could earn enough to build a home for his family and to furnish it. The Reyes finally had their own bedstead, a majestic art-piece of five different woods, handmade and polished by Benji himself.

His insistence on quality and perfection has earned him recognition. In the late 1990s he was invited to join the fringe of the annual FAME show. When several curators spotted his unique works, he found his marketing niche. Today three galleries carry his chairs: Gallery 139, Lopez Museum shop and Firma. Proud owners of his distinctive, sensuous-lined, oil-rubbed works refer to them as their Benji Reyes—"in the same tone as a Bencab or Luz".

Left: The staircase's wavy wooden banister is a modern art master-piece in their midst. Reyes's woody creations guides one all the way down four levels of this unique home.

Overleaf: Rustic dining in an earthy and artsy kitchen. It's all wood and stone, everywhere; with bamboo and craftsy paper for candle-holders. It took 12 years before the wood-artist could earn enough to build a home for his family—along with every stick of furniture within it.

Right: The sun sets over Manila Bay—and the last of the romantic views above Roxas Boulevard. Netz is quick to boast of his bayside flat, which affords this unique view of the sunset. He shares his space with a giant tribal ritual figure and an array of creative crafts and moderne furnishings

Outré Ethnicity

Cluttered or organic? Or just eccentric and eclectic? The decor trip moves back to a casual and cluttered style—as interpreted by an eccentric arts and crafts collector in Manila. Writer Stephen Long described this look in *World of Interiors* as the cluttered style that is "not a contrived scheme or method, but more often a combination of beautiful and idiosyncratic items, which come together to create a highly personal scenario which would be a nightmare to move."

The flat's resident, Bernard Knut Netz, is a German consultant to CITEM, the government's trade exhibitions agency. He's an avowed lover of individualist Filipino modern art and pop-camp kitsch. Netz is also an avid collector of new organic crafts and furniture and a generally eccentric and artsy bohemian dweller of Malate. The effusive consultant is quick to boast about his apartment— first for its superb view of the sunset over Manila Bay and then for the array of unique and interesting furnishings that provide comfortable companions for viewing the evening spectacle.

This Malate apartment was decorated by sheer happenstance and personal idiosyncracy. Netz had craved this flat for its unbeatable view, then pursued the space from the previous expat resident—even offering to buy the heavy wood and stone monoliths then used as furniture! Today a huge, boat-like log sserves as the sofa and a giant prehistoric stone is the coffeetable. The owner's desk and work area are

defined by a giant wooden sugar-cane grinder—complete but for the carabao, water buffalo—on which are mounted several bizarre Hindu-ritualist artworks by modern sculptor, Gabby Barredo. Most of the small guestroom is occupied by an entire life-sized *calesa* (carriage), sans horse, but trimmed with sparkling Christmas lights lining the main frame.

Apart from the love of crafts, tribal weavings, and folksy paintings, the special feature of the Netz's home is the unexpected mix of Filipino-designed furniture which takes pride of place for watching the proverbial sunset. He recently acquired the now-famous Yin and Yang cubist armchair by Cebu-based designer Kenneth Cobonpue, with its metal frame wrapped with open-weave rattan. The airy cubic masterpiece joins two organic wood creations by Antipolo-based designer Benji Reyes—a wavy screen and oil-finished rocking chair. At Manila's cocktail hour, Netz toasts the spectacular sunset and, as he is quick to add, the "best three Filipino artists: Benji Reyes, Gabby Barredo and Kenneth Cobonpue".

Above: The Netz apartment was decorated by happenstance as one eccentric collector followed upon a previous one. Today a huge (immovable) hull-like wood monolith serves as the sofa, ornamented with ethnic fabric cushions; while an antique grinding stone or ritual vessel comprises the coffeetable. The mixed media painting, "Sangre Azul" (Blue Blood), is by Mario de Rivera.

Left: Most of the guestroom space is occupied by an entire *calesa* (carriage)—sans horse, but complete with Christmas lights lining the main frame (not shown). On the other side of the room is this charming window collage painting by an unknown artist. Shell-lamps are by Disegno en Asia, Cebu. The waxed paper umbrella in the foreground is from Thailand.

Right: Netz is an ebullient artsy bohemian dweller of Malate as well as a lover of individualist Filipino modern art. One favourite artist is Benji Reyes, whose signature rocking chair and wavy screen divider mellow in the afternoon light. In the corner, a tall bamboo and paper lamp by Wendy Regalado is suspended from the ceiling.

Opposite, clockwise from top left: Resin decor balls embedded with bleached coco-chips, shells, vines and twigs. A rounded resin tray striped with coconut fibre motifs. *Gaddang* tribal weaves from the north accent giant floor pillows. The weathered grinder hub makes a textured tabletop. A black keepsake box is laminated and pressed with whole bamboo leaves. This ceremonial ornament from Bontoc is made of a whole Mother of Pearl shell.

Fusion and Fantasy

Laguna resident Ernest Santiago is a silver-haired magus and the compleat designer, forever fantasizing and designing whatever gets into his head or hands. During the 1970s he was Santiago de Manila (his couturier signature), leading the fashion scene and known for his bold silhouettes and strong presence. As a fashion impresario in the '80s, he designed the outrageous disco, Coco Banana. When he finally tired of the city, he moved to the *probinsiya*, to Pagsanjan in the riverine province of Laguna. There he delved into all-natural furniture design, making classic Chinese-style chairs from gnarled bamboo, incorporating river stones, sugar grinders and molave wood railway ties into his creative home and jungled garden.

By the '90s Santiago evolved from landscape and furniture designer into a creative architect of weekend retreats outside Manila. Conjuring uniquely tropical and rustic, naturalist and minimalist interiors, he quietly become the chic designer for the elite.

For three decades Ernest Santiago has been riding a post-modern Filipino design wave of his own making. Drawing on Laguna's rivers, vegetation and florid antique houses he absorbs Nature's vivid influences.

Santiago has recently designed a fantasy abode in his back garden: three tropical pavilions interpreting Asian-Fusion themes for a creative dweller. He calls the first pavilion Boya (buoys). The open-air gazebo features glass buoys, wooden angels and grinder stones 'flying' from a trellis among the leaves. Cobalt blue ceramic pedestals provide chairs for languid brunches and *meriendas*.

Above: The Filipino Pavilion features a native headman's rustic quarters under an A-frame *nipa* roof. The natural wood daybed, The River, was made from solid *narra*, a giant molave branch, and three riverstones as joinery. The towering terracotta floor lamp is made from several antique water sewer pipes. The white silk drapery and vines are photogenic strokes from the master.

The Pinoy (Filipino) pavilion is a native A-frame hut with a thatched *nipa* roof. Santiago's wood and stone divan, The River, bears an embracing molave branch as its backrest. The tall floor lamp was made from terracotta water pipes. The green glass lantern was purchased at Arte Espanol.

Finally, the Pan-Asian Temple is a cogon-thatched, walled pavilion in deep-rose, raised over a pond, with water gurgling from a low-lying stone fountain (fashioned from Thai cooking stoves). Santiago's dual-headed Khmer warrior (a copy he had custom carved) guards the pavilion near a pebble garden and Thai spirit house complete with thatched-roof. Within, a Thai-Filipino *papag* (daybed) is turned into a regal divan, surrounded with low tables and painted seats. The pavilion's glowing, gilded centrepiece is an antique Tibetan altar, replete with

erotic dancing gods and animals; he calls it a "celebration of passion and fertility". The narrow bamboo staircase with banister leads to a sleeping loft above. Eventually, Santiago de Manila plans to offer his fantasy compound as an exotic getaway for visitors in Pagsanjan.

Till then, irrepressible Santiago is still collecting and collating vivid influences from the world around him—especially from Bangkok's Chatuchak Weekend Market with its dazzling Asian treasures. The Filipino magus is still reeling too under the influence of New York City's latest Cirque du Soleil spectacle, Dra-lion. The theatrical show, replete with airborne spirits and wraiths, has turned his dizzy Dragon head! Someday, Santiago vows, he will create something so big and mind-boggling—just to show Filipinos what living design can be!

Left and above: Santiago de Manila designs even stones and stoves! His own water fountain sculpture comprises several Thai stone cooking stoves, unified under a stone globe. The gurgling pool forms a moat around the large Thai-Balinese-Tibetan pavilion.

Opposite: The theatrical Pan-Asian pavilion glows with myriad cultures and deities. On the main floor one lounges by a gilded Tibetan altar which is a "celebration of passion and fertility". Up the bamboo staircase one sleeps in an open loft closer to heaven. The wide, rustic seat near the altar is Santiago's interpretation of a Chinese imperial chair in Philippine bamboo.

Above: A most regal *papag* (divan) for kingly aspirations in Laguna. The traditional cane-woven daybed has been recycled and recreated with wood-carved details from ornate Philippine and Thai furnishings. The gilded pillows and fan, low footstools and silver dragon dish are from Bangkok's weekend market.

Right: The ever-romantic designer enjoys this colourful cocoon of fibres and fabrics, erected on a hill of San Mateo. With bamboo groves and mango trees as surroundings, she invites nature inside, to share the open-air, bamboo-rimmed back terrace. Gauzy drapery made of banana hemp and rayon fabric is air-brushed with the colours of the elements.

Earthly Haven

A wholesome home is a refuge from the stresses of the outside world, a restful place that nurtures, calms, relaxes. The home haven should indulge the senses and sensitivities, be rich with tactile pleasures, and closely link the dweller with nature and the healing power of plants.

A personal refuge amidst nature is exactly what fashion designer Dita Sandico Ong has created in a three-level *bahay-kubo* (thatched house) on the north eastern edge of Manila—in the last rainforest she could find. This calm cocoon, as she describes it, indulges her romantic nature and fuels her creativity, stimulating her work with fabrics and fashion.

Ong brings both earthly wisdom and whimsy to the thoroughly rustic space. Nature lingers within the open-sided tree house, extends through the varied rooms that branch off from a central wooden staircase and are constructed on three levels. A bamboo grove forms a front curtain walls, a leafy barrier provides dappled shade and privacy. Criss-crossed bamboo trellises, fashioned by artist friends, become wall panels. In selected spots, her own pastel-toned paintings function as wallpapers, applied directly on smooth, white cemented surfaces by the staircase, in the hallway, and in the shower nook—where a naif flower garden painting evokes bathing on a tropical island. Far below, Ong has created a outdoor dining nook by raising a circular wall of bamboo poles and recycling naturally hewn wooden planks and trunks as the rustic furnishings.

Above: Oversized bamboo latticework and natural woods are practical furnishings in a hot-climate *bahay*. Lattices of natural branches, some filled in with vinework, form the room's see-through walls. A giant molave trunk makes a daybed; a sugar mill hub and cartwheel. The hanging panel and throw-pillow were painted by crafts-man Darwin Chua.

Left: **Peaceful meditation is guaranteed within this tactile organic interior. The bamboo-clad prayer corner within the designer's bedroom unites the elements of earth and air; water, wood and nature.**

Below: **Picturesque bedroom under the *anahaw* palm roof. The holistic resident indulges romance in her sleeping quarters. Blue and white *iloco-abel* fabric is her bed linen, fine muslin cloth is the bed's drapery; red cloth flowers coddle a table lamp.**

Her bedroom and the upper *sala* are languid spaces decorated with cool muslin drapery; bed linen in blue-and-white *Iloco-abel* fabric; and hand-painted banana-fibre panels. Meanwhile, Mother Nature's own shadows, textures and reflections shine upon her tiny meditation rock altar, set against a bamboo pole background. Ong finds it hard to return to the urban rat race after each weekend spent in her bahay cocoon.

In *World of Interiors*, designer John Stefandis described the idyllic Hot Climate Style: "It is equal parts romanticism, sensuality and practicality. It is a way of appreciating the simple life. It is architecture without architects: furnishings are countrified, handmade and not too grand. Living in a hot country reawakens the senses. There is tactile romance in going barefoot. There are those restful colours, pastels even, the traditional blue, pale pink, melon, light gray and lime green. The greatest pleasure is being out of doors. Rooms open on to terraces and pleasure gardens surrounded by tropical plants." A more apt description of Ong's *bahay* life would be hard to find.

Right: The designer plays throughout her three-level *bahay* space and hand-paints her retainer walls to indulge her painterly senses. The outdoor stairway landing has a cement surface that has become willing canvas for Dita's signature images.

Left: A dining room outdoors means going back to the basics: a privacy wall of natural bamboo poles and split molave logs for benches. "Plus always, there is organic food—for thought and for eating," says the holistic Dita. "So when people leave the space, they're changed and recharged."

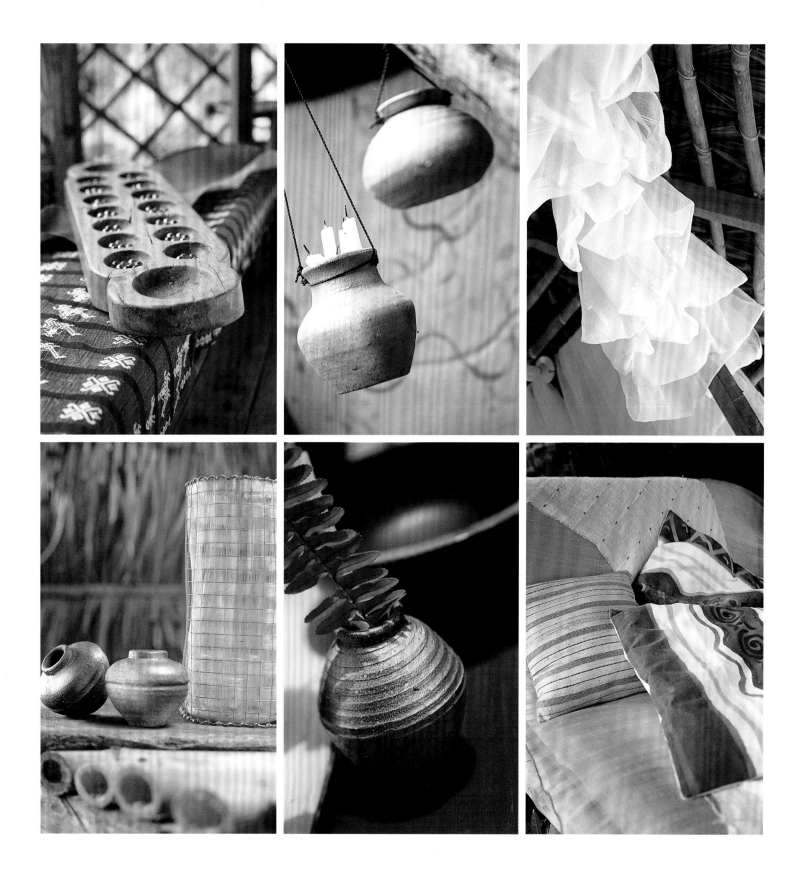

Opposite: The tactile pleasures of the *bahay*, shown clockwise from top left: *Sunkaan*, the Chinese wooden board game (now filled with blue marbles) sits upon a blue horse-themed blanket from Ilocos. Miniature *burnay* pots from Vigan (i.e. fired in a traditional wood-burning kiln) are hung and strung about as candleholders. Swathes of white muslin are gathered and festooned overhead, for a fresh fluffy effect. Natural fabrics made of banana-hemp and painted with modern colours animate the space. A small *burnay* jarlet is touched up with a spray of silver; behind is a hardwood *kamagong* bowl. A cylindrical candleholder is created from gilded chicken wire and banana fabric lining.

Right: Luminous soft furnishings by fabric designer Elisa Reyes. This innovative self-taught weaver from Bulacan creates modern fabrics for fashion manufacturers, using banana (*abaca*) fibre, combined with rayon, linen, and *buri* palm. For 10 years, she has marketed designer placemats in contemporary colours to Europe and the USA. (She is known to the House of Armani and the Elsa Klensch Show.) The blue-to-yellow wet-look lampshade and palm-patterned textile were created by craftsman Darwin Chua.

Tropical
Urban

The 'moderne' style is manifested here in
cutting-edge designs and sleek, sophisticated
lines that remain natural, and functional.
Designers combine a modernist sensibility and
an Asian sensitivity to natural materials.

Previous page, top row, middle: **Tripods by Corita Yu for Techmasters, Cebu.**

Left: **The condo's abundance is showcased with Zen-like balance. Chinese traditional furnishing is synchronized with Asian modern art, by Romulo Olazo; modern Japanese print by Toko Shinoda; and a pivotal oil, "Neurotic Zen Master", by Lao Lianben. The bamboo vases and violet organza cushions are from Kish at Glorietta.**

Artful Zen

A simple style implies not a lack of sophistication but a clean, balanced and essential way. As designer Terence Conran wrote in *World of Interiors*, "SIMPLE perfectly describes an overall approach to interiors, where there's an especially strong sense of design, where each of the elements must relate to everything else in the room. There's a positive delight in strong lines; and a preference for things that are puritanical, rustic, natural and functional."

Simple, clean lines characterize the Rockwell apartment belonging to Jose and Tina Quiros. The low-key lady of the condominium, Tina Quiros, had already bought her collection of classic Chinese furniture from antiques dealer, Ruby Nazir, of Noble House. Jose 'Bebo' Quiros, an inveterate collector, was reluctant to have anyone 'design' his collection of Filipino modern art; so the couple asked Ivy Almario to arrange their existing furnishings in a simple style, "very clean, very Zen-like".

Ivy and Associates (Almario works with an all-female staff) have been making waves in the new condominiums at Rockwell and at last count have done some 22 apartments in the complex. Almario's forte is not that of one defined style, but rather the ability to interpret a client's vision. "Essentially, we become design editors," she explains, "When there is abundance we exercise restraint; but in restraint there must also be abundance. As designers we develop the expertise to achieve that balance."

"Most hard-set and proud art collectors wouldn't entrust their homes to anyone else but themselves," comments Quiros, but he admits that Almario's fine-tuned styling allows him to enjoy

Right: Galloping Oriental horses in several dimensions hover about the Tang-inspired dining area, while an expansive mirror reflects upon the Quiros' serene, all-Chinese themed flat.

Below: The black-stained cane *escritoryo* (writing desk) by E. Murio Designs is paired with a restful, abstract work by Pep Manalang.

Far Left: Designer Ivy Almario distilled bold-scaled furniture and simple modern forms to provide visual impact in the den. The space is dominated by a giant portrait by expressionist Onib Olmedo.

Left: The designer's sure moves direct the eye to the outer terrace: a rustic bench and low seat from Ifugao are topped off with a giant wooden cartwheel, which resembles a Chinese coin.

and share his enthusiasms. A connoisseur of Filipino art, Quiros spends his leisure time talking art and artists, enjoying the cigar-bar at the Mandarin and nurturing his collection. "I told Ivy she could design the condo, provided I am not separated from my paintings! She did a good job. The artworks are very alive and still talking to me." And this includes the *sala's* enduring centrepiece, "Neurotic Zen Master", an early work by Lao Lianben.

Almario used a gentle hand to conjure a quiet new space with perfect balance and serenity. She nurtured the surfaces using thick *abaca* weave carpets, raffia textured wall coverings and drapes, and erected false, display walls to add depth and dimension. She highlighted with details that pull together furnishings and objects such the Asian modern ecru-shaded lamp and the Thai-made violet organza pillows. And she used the exotic flower arrangements— provided weekly by Tina Quiros's country gardener—as those essential accents.

Right: **Four-square, bold and modern—a compact composition in blacks, beiges and Cordillera ethnica. Laurena's sitting room centres round a four-piece modular coffeetable, grounding his European inspired furnishings and Philippine ethnic artefacts collection.**

Contemporary Ethnic

Interior designer Roland Laurena mixes classical style and modern sensibility with professional ease. A seasoned designer and craftsman, Laurena is best known for his exotic textured finishes, a look that was lauded as being way ahead of its time. In the mid-80s, while consulting on crafts for CITEM, the government trade expositions centre, Laurena tapped world trends and introduced new styles and materials to the local market. He developed fresh techniques which included handcrafting moulded stone from ground coral rock and coloured shells, using skins (including eel, stingray, lizard and pigskin) for unusual accessories, fashioned novel finishes for furniture and accents, and worked with leather.

This texture master was also recognized for his innovative furniture design inspired by period European furniture. For instance, he revamped the Louis XV armchair by covering it with monitor lizard skin—and, unsurprisingly, caught the international eye. In 1992, as the Filipino design consultant for Eli Mansor's CITEM, he taught local manufacturers how to create simple works with basic design principles not, as he underlined, "designers' additions". Cebu, he acknowledged, has a wealth of natural, raw materials but the skill in keeping its myriad crafts alive lies not in saturating a market with over-adorned items, but by instilling solid design concepts and the ability to adapt to market trends.

TRIBAL
SCULPTURE

Laurena has recently settled into a sleek, modern condominium work of architect Lor Calma. In this new space, he merges his late 1990s' design experience with chrome, aluminium, stainless steel and dark *wenge* wood with his love for ethnic traditions and textures. An indulgence, perhaps, but he proudly displays his Cordillera baskets, *bulols* (spirit figures) and wooden spoons. "In the 1970s, I was obsessed with collecting something that's *atin*, our very own. I collected small ethnic artefacts just to appreciate their form. Then I would design a modular frame for them, to give importance to even the smallest item."

He is still framing ethnic forms in his compact modern space. His square modular coffeetable is a designer work of dark and light—solid wood and glass, featuring electric lights. Cabinets and display cases for Ifugao tribal artworks double as room dividers. His colours are bold, masculine and stable: black-*wenge*, browns and beiges. "I'm an earth sign, Taurus, so I can't leave the browns and blacks." Yet Laurena remains the incurable eclectic: "I still like to mix classic and ethnic styles," he explains. "I'd like to be all modern and minimal, but I can't. I enjoy many ethnic things and love textures around me."

Above: **Black is beautiful. This artefacts corner displays niches and benches for ethnic collections—antique black basket from Bontoc; a seated *bulol* (rice god image); carved spoons from Ifugao; stone-veneered lamp by Leo Almeria; and a modernist acrylic artwork by Lee Aguinaldo.**

Left: Making room for a view. *Wenge*-black cabinets divide the space in the living room into functional areas, and display myriad artefacts and art *objets*. The skin-covered pear is a Laurena signature. The two balls near the floor are carved from Mt. Pinatubo's volcanic ash.

Opposite: Laurena designed his black *wenge* wood dining table after a Balinese altar table, which exudes a fire-light from the centre. The small square room is uplifted by four modern dining chairs, two standing Ifugao *bulols* (deity figures), and three 19th-century botanical prints by Father Manuel Blanco.

Below: Twin *bulol* (rice god) figures perched atop a Cordillera ritual box—an unusual wood piece from Laurena's favourite tribal collections.

Bottom: A chalice stoneware dish from Cardinal Ceramics.

Above: Laurena's planes and pears. The modern condo with openings sans mouldings features a floating console table—to underline the owner's favoured ethnic accents and *objets:* pigskin pears and abstract paintings.

Opposite: Yin & Yang armchairs by Kenneth Cobonpue, of Interior Crafts of the Islands, Cebu. The cubist metal framework is intricately wrapped with rattan splits.

Right: The showroom is all white and open, with expanses of glass windows inviting in the garden view. Milo Naval of Evolve Designs creates massive, boldly modern, *abaca* plaited forms; modular furnishings with an individual mentality and attitude.

Movement 8 Moderne

When something is called 'modern' it generally means it is from this era, this time, now. But Modern can also point to the design movement that grew out of 1920s Modernism—as author Suzanne Trocme traces in *Influential Interiors*: "In America the Moderne style combined art-deco and a restrained modernism featuring a startling geometrically, patterned form. By 1926 Streamlined Moderne evolved from both art-deco and the Bauhaus. Furniture was low, simple and horizontal, based on fundamental shapes: rectangle, circle and triangle. Lines were sleek. Materials included brass, chrome and aluminium, rather than wood."

The Philippines' claim to the Modern, Moderne and Modernist sensibility is a design consortium called Movement 8—referring to a loose society of all-modernist designers who have hitched their creative wagons to the international trade show circuit. Spearheaded by CITEM (Center for International Trade Expositions and Missions) chief Eli Pinto Mansor and edited and directed by Budji Layug, Manila's most successful designer in recent years, the Movement 8 trade exhibitions have been winning accolades at every world design show since Fall 1999 with their first overseas appearance in Valencia, Spain. After just three foreign 'outings',

Left: This rounded seat and ottoman wear rustic textures over their sleek modern form. The maverick designer is Kenneth Cobonpue of Interior Crafts of the Islands, Cebu.

Below: Glass-topped accent table, by Cebu FilVeneer. The wooden boxes are laminated with striated patterns of vines amid black resin, by industrial designer Louisa Robinson.

Opposite: An amazing topiary chaise, Pigalle. This rounded designer chair hearkens to a modern sculpture or a low-slung sports car, by Kenneth Cobonpue for Interior Crafts of the Islands, Cebu. Nearby, Tess Pasola's paper artwork shines like a layered grey moon; over two striped brown resin vases by Louisa Robinson. The fringed pillow is by Catalina's, Cebu.

the Filipino delegation was invited to join the top furniture shows of Europe. By May 2001, after strutting their stuff in the International Contemporary Furniture Fair in New York, USA, Movement 8 took home the prestigious top award for crafts-manship; and garnered features in major US interior magazines. This designers' society that made its impact abroad has recently found a permanent show-case in Makati, in the B-at-Home showroom, owned and designed by Movement 8 director, Budji Layug.

The B-at-Home showroom, writes *PD Inquirer* Editor Thelma San Juan, "is a minimalist showcase of the world-class cutting-edge designs of Filipino artists known as Movement 8, all of whom have been shepherded by CITEM." All the furniture and home accents blend into one integrated whole—without clutter and pretense. You see home masterpieces cast in modernist functional design, much of it innovative and trail-blazing. The showroom serves as these artists' retail outlet, while their works are treated as an integral part of a home and a design philosophy."

Says Layug of the wide, white setting: "Embellishment must have a reason. Design must have logic, rhythm and flow. Every space needs

Opposite, clockwise from top left: The wiry oval seat by Davao-based Ann Pamintuan of The Gilded Expressions is an edgy sculpture that has won accolades in the West. Three tripod candle holders dance on stainless toes; metal work by Noel Sadicon of Technopoint. Two vases exude a smart organic look; resin art by Louisa Robinson. An anthropomorphic stone sculpture by modern artist Impy Pilapil came for a show and stayed. Cobonpue's low centred Pigalle *chaise* (Movement 8's attention-getter of 2001) comprises a steel framework, structured like tracery, wrapped in *abaca* twine—it's a true merging of modernist technology and Asian natural materials and craftsmanship.

Right: Minimalist chairs and equine arts. Spare and simple meeting chairs balance on steely frames—with refined chic to spare; by Budji Layug for B-at-Home Gallery. Modernist iron horse dances in the white light of the space; metal sculpture by Royston Taylor of Alabang.

Opposite: The modernist showroom expressed as a home. Designer Budji Layug's philosophy of harmony and integreation is executed in low, simple and horizontal furnishings, subdued earth colours and modern accessories.

Left: Sleeping with the modernists. Movement 8's upstairs bedroom set comprises a mat-inspired contemporary bedstead by Budji Layug; and a wide, square lounger seat wrapped in plaited *abaca* rope, by architect-turned-furniture designer, Milo Naval.

Below: A glass topped round-the-corner accent table for books, artworks and conversation starters, by Carlo Cordaro of Cebu FilVeneer Co. The wiggly wood accessory is by nature artist Claude Tayag.

integration and harmony of line and shape, or material, texture, and accent." Layug's own furniture echoes the modern lines of Mies van der Rohe, interpreted in natural weaves. Milo Naval, one of the bestsellers in the group, displays a grand scaled, modular dining room, set with white Japanese crockery. Recent accolades have shone on the airy, cubist armchairs by Kenneth Cobonpue. His see-through Yin & Yang armchair is a metal framework intricately wrapped with rattan splits. The rounded lounger, Pigalle, is a curvy *chaise* composed of wiry steel bound in *abaca* twine. Cobonpue provides the best take on Movement 8's Philippine moderne: "We're all designers who share the same belief in the mixture of a modernist sensibility and an Asian sensitivity to craftsmanship and natural materials."

Left: Bernie Sason's black leather and bamboo sofa is paired with his moderne ottoman. On the left wall is a red and black abstract by Florencio Concepcion, while on the right panel hangs a grey and white composite by Lao Lianben. In the middle of the room sits an outre red-rose floral sculpture by Tony Padilla. At floor level are black *banig* pillows from Tesoro's and marble egg sculptures by artist Impy Pilapil.

Functional Arts

Curator Albert Avellana channels his experience with art objects to directing photography of homes for print. After styling so many homes, Avellana decided to bring modern art and houses together. He directs young artists towards the notion of 'functional art', and explains: "I want to push the term 'art' off the wall, push artists to create works for everyday use. Help art to be accepted as utilitarian. And show artists there's no denigration in doing functional things nor in being considered a craftsman, like Impy Pilapil and Claude Tayag."

Avellana found an old Pasay house to contain his idea. He took over the 1936 home of fashion-manufacturer, Larry Silva, complete with high ceilings, wide wood floors, plaster columns, French doors, and iron grillwork straight out of art deco. The curator proceeded to realign the genteel old space to work as a retro-modern gallery for functional arts.

He applied basic principles from the art gallery, replanning the overall layout and providing space around art objects. He created new openings, new sitting areas, and transferred the front entrance to occur at the end of a processional. To counter-balance the dark wood floors, he added false white 'museum walls' in selected areas. The interiors lit up immediately, giving the old house its modern feel. Spotlights were arranged and the first modern artworks were placed.

Below: Artist and craftsman Claude Tayag's wood-art corner. An angular and twisted artwork dances at the foot of a medicine chest-cum-sundries cabinet, while a red and black tribal ethnic painting by Ivi Cosio perches on the wall.

Right: Four towers of coconut disk candlesticks topped off by tealights, designed by architect Reimon Gutierrez. The painting behind the coco-towers is an oil abstract by Florencio Concepcion.

Outside sat the retro-Memphis chairs and tables by glass artist Impy Pilapil. In the front room stood functional sculptures by wood-artist Claude Tayag and coconut tealight holders by Reimon Gutierrez. Inside, Avellana mounted large paintings by Ivi Cosio, Lao Lianben, Florencio Concepcion and Eugene Jarque. "When you start with big art with deep messages or visual impact," Avellana says, "You're 60 per cent of the way to a good-spirited space!"

Avellana then outfitted the rooms with modern rustic furniture designs to compliment the artworks. He chose functional and flexible furniture—items that are smart, modern and crafted from local materials—creating designs with inherent impact. These include Bernie Sason's eclectic chairs, which combine black leather with crushed bamboo in a bold, individualist style reminiscent of Art Deco, and Tesoro's bamboo settee, made from whole poles combined with industrial tubing. Avellana developed other functional works from artist friends including Noel Farol's three-legged dining table with lizards etched under the glass, and interior designer Manny Castro's one-of-a-kind table, from Antipolo, combining a pink fossil-stone top from Cebu with art-deco wooden legs. Finally, there's the doormat artwork by Christina Valdezco; it functions as a floor rug, a giant tapestry or just a conversation piece.

Left: The *comedor* (dining room) by the 1936 staircase. Artsy dining takes place at a three-legged glass table with *butiki* (lizards) etched beneath, created by Noel Farol, and black leather and wood disked chairs by maverick designer Bernie Sason of Bacolod. In counterpoint is the silvery mixed-media mural by Eugene Jarque. The large glass presentation dish is by Bobby Castillo, while the traditional sheer *piña* tablecloth is courtesy of Tesoro's, and the golden floral accent is by Tony Padilla.

Below: Off-the-wall artworks for on-the-floor functions. In this children's room, foot rugs enjoined by artist Mac Valdezco become a carpet tapestry. The soft stuffed sculptures by the pedestal are by Alma Quinto, while the light box on two branches is by Belgian artist Hilde Orye. From Tesoro's: placemats, mat-weave pillows and Pinatubo-ash coffee set. The stone candleholder by Zambrox.

Right: Contemporary glass trays and serving dishes by Bobby Castillo, functional art displayed at the Avellana Gallery.

Right, bottom: An arty ante-room setting. The vertical grey and white painting by Lao Lianben balances above a bow-legged console table by wood craftsman, Ting Gonzalez of Patina. On the table is a four-tier lightbox by Hilde Orye.

Opposite: The room gets its tribal spirit from a giant painting of ethnic inspiration by Ivi Cosio. Furniture goes mod-organic with two whole-bamboo settees on aluminium tube legs, and placemats and bowls from Tesoro's, Manila. The pink-stoned coffeetable is a collab-orative work designed by Manny Castro, and the tall glass presentation dish is by craftsman Bobby Castillo.

Left: The old front porch turns comfortably modern with its artworks, from the "Headless Rider" art installation in blue glass armour by Bobby Castillo, to the two-toned, two textured sculptural marble vase on the ledge by Impy Pilapil. Flying in between is a glass angel, also by Castillo. Wood benches are curator-stylist Avellana's vintage flea market finds.

Below: Playful spirits ring the old house in the modern setting by artist Impy Pilapil. A retro-Memphis chair with her water themed glass signature on the chair back sits proudly by a glass and stone table composite: a pink marble ball and white marble column balance upon a natural rock-slab base. Behind that is Pilapil's "Seed"—a feather-shaped sculpture in heavy bronze.

Tropical Eclectic

Eclecticism in interior design involves 'mixing polarities'—assembling unique, idiosyncratic, and even theatrical and exotic items. The effusive settings here bespeak the wit and flair of the designer—and they work!

Mexican Madness

Some houses are wholeheartedly eccentric. Style-writer Elizabeth Wilhide put it best: "The people who create them follow no fashions, adhere to no rules, and are above criticism; their houses are a genuine key to their characters. The owners exhibit an unbounded, self-indulgent confidence in their own taste, caring not for the opinion of others."

Eccentric decoration is not a style but a state of mind. Such decorators are individualists to whom originality comes naturally and their anarchic interiors, fizzing with energy and joy, are an antidote to what is safe and conventional. The result is vibrant, quirky and not to everyone's taste.

A Mexican house in Quezon City, home and office of an ultra-creative Filipino, epitomizes this eccentricity. For four years he has been working

on his home and, as the neighbourhood develops, has retreated into a fabulous fantasy world of his own making. This irreverent and creative soul loves wild and artful things and has no use for simple forms and undecorated surfaces. He collects anything witty, funky or interesting; gathers fine artworks by his friends, and popsicle-coloured folk art by a little 80-year-old lady of Pampanga. He adores hot Mexican colours in folk crafts and surrreal images in fine arts, but he doesn't hang his abundant paintings conventionally—he props them up on tables, and lines walls and floors, three deep.

His passion, however, does not stop there: this Pinoy (Filipino) eclectic is also fascinated by mythical horses and merry-go-rounds, frog figurines and pre-Columbian pots from Batangas. By painting

Above: Welcome to the Flintstones Room, a boulder-lined, colourful *sala*. The central classic rocks painting is by Lamarossa. Excavated Batangas pottery and ceramics line the back wall. In the middle of the room is a blue and aqua distressed-finish *baul* (trunk), now 'camouflaged' as coffeetable.

Opposite: This lusciously Mexican-inspired *tromp-l'oeil* door features a cobalt blue jamb framing a yellow-green door with distressed finish. The folksy painted vinework is by Al Cortes and the decoupage art is by Cabiling.

Right: The back room has cabinets for the family silver, and tangerine walls for Filipino paintings. There's an awesome feast for the eyes, especially in the early works by modern master Jose Joya. Note the spotted-cat armchair, ultimate kitsch from the '80s. The resident merrily mixes and matches. "I love to show that a room can be all mixed and eclectic with lots of Pinoy things—and can be beautiful!"

Left: Even the overspill of collectibles in the garage expresses the owner's eccentric taste and love of nature. An old *platera* or glass cabinet displays antique ceramics against bright orange walls and a painted window set-design that gazes outward to a lush flower garden! The chimera atop the cabinet is a horse-dragon-fish out of Philippine folklore.

Below: The technicoloured foyer frames a child's rocking horse. At the far end is a terracotta altarpiece, "Mama Mary of Guadalupe", a unique creation by unschooled folk artist Ebeng Sibog from Bulacan. Behind is an apt and airy airbrushed painting by Danilo Garcia. Vine-patterned 'cadena' tiles border the floor. Lining the walls are surreal modern paintings by Fernando Modesto, Nestor Vinluan, Norberto Carating.

trompe l'oeil landscapes on the walls of each room, he creates fantasy themes for his collection. There are Flintstone rocks in the *sala* and a tropical *gubat* (forest) growing in the back bedroom under a slanted roof. Recently the house made it into the TV special, "Awesome Interiors".

In the past, he and his partners have designed modern furniture and been offered big orders but he's not tempted to travel that route. He explains: "We're just artists doing creative things; we don't want to expand and run a business."

This eccentric homeowner has travelled to Bali and Bangkok, where he thrills at new, modern crafts. But he really adores all things Mexican. "Because of the Galleon trade," he reasons, "there was so much fusion of colour that it became part of the Filipino perception. So the Pinoy likes his life and space *makulay*, colourful."

Multicoloured perceptions begin at the front door, a Mexican-inspired concoction in *tromp-l'oeil* with a crown of vines emerging from a tomato-red wall. Peeping inside, one is mesmerized within by the arts and crafts profusion on folkloric altars in every corner. Whatever the season, the awesome Pinoy-Mexican interiors fizz with energy and joy— and a little madness.

Right: Outrageous scale plays its huge hand. The compact dining space expands in the big mirror wall and shows off varied Filipino craftsmanship. The mirror is hand-etched with Philippine flora, while flowers bloom in Granny's *ganchillo* (crocheted) table-cloth. The real-sized carousel horse is a folk-art piece, just one treasure from the mad collector's stable (of horses and frogs).

Below: The homeowner amasses all things wild and beautiful. These candlesticks were concocted from dis-carded salt and pepper shakers sandwiched between resin components. Other inventive decor items (not shown) were made from recycled soy-sauce bottles and tooth-pick shakers.

Opposite: A multi-deity display on a green hollow-block wall. Here hang the owner's folksy array of *bahay-santo* (carved home altars for saint-figures) from Bohol, along-side theatre masks from Bali, to watch over him while he sleeps. The couch is draped with a silken throw made of *saya* (women's skirt) frag-ments, created by fabric artist and stylist Steve de Leon.

Right: The Balinese *gubat* (forest) bedroom has emerged from the house's former garage. Production artist Dan Clarissa painted the "Green Mansions" forest with jungle leaves and vines snaking about, overgrowing the space. The "Harrassed Naked Man" figure is a resin sculpture by Vicaldo. Behind, an abstract painting by Roy Veneracion.

Below: The marine-themed 'head' or fishy Comfort Room (toilet), painted by Al Cortes. Walls are fully illustrated and animated with plants, drift-wood, fish and seaweed. Relief works in terracotta and free-swimming fish works are by Quezon's most creative potter, Ugu Bigyan.

Philippine Élan

Among these varied pages, the middle-class home of Gerico and Baby Austria is the most personal, nationalistic, and charmingly folksy. The home contains the ethnic wood collection of a much-travelled marketing man—a vast array of artefacts gathered during his forays among the islands. The Austrias had long gathered old wood and dreamed of their own fresh version of an all-Filipino home. Designer Eric Paras assisted them in creating their own "self-portrait", a task requiring a perceptive and personable approach.

Today the house exterior looks Mediterranean: pale yellow stucco walls, rounded arches, high tiled roofs and inner spaces full of light from soaring glass windows. The house was scaled to encompass the large wooden pieces and architectural details—carved panels, balusters, roughhewn railway ties. Paras accommodated old molave trunks (as house-posts);

ten-foot wooden ritual drums from Zamboanga (as decor); and a dozen-odd antique doors (as whatever possible).

There are no name-brand furniture lines here; just traditional wood pieces by unnamed native craftsmen. Almost every stick of furniture—chosen by the Austrias' eye for heritage things—is a fine Filipino form: the *balayong* wood trestle table for dining; long work benches plus a slatted *gallinera* (seat with a chicken coop) as dinner chairs. The open-plan dining alcove is 'carpeted' with a span of bright-hued, retro-patterned tiles by Machuca ceramics, a salute to olden art-deco tiles.

Baby Austria's big kitchen is the delightful warm hearth and favourite family nook. Paras did a 'distressed' treatment on blue and yellow-painted cupboards and built Mrs Austria a rustic oven alcove

Above: **The delectable breakfast nook is a family favourite spot in the house. This white-curtained corner looks out through a bay window onto a scenic backyard with pool and fountain. Traditional Philippine armchairs, muslin curtains with shell and macrame tie-backs, and a Dutch lamp in milkglass impart graciousness to the setting.**

Left: The Austrias' home moves to the beat of a different drummer—the home-owner's collection of wooden drums, including several 10-foot ritual drums from Maranao. The atrium *sala* soars with natural light pouring in through high arched windows. A bright aqua contemporary sofa chair (from Art Fab) is juxtaposed against the woody-earthy Filipiniana decor.

Above: The Austrias' fresh and rustic dining hall is unified by a wide carpet of amber and blue Machuca tiles that complement the woody hues. The dining chairs comprise a simple long bench and a slatted *gallinera* (rural seat made for storing live chickens beneath), straddling a trestle table. Note the antique oil lamp, birdcages from Hong Kong, and four-foot candlesticks converted from old *mulion* (carved window supports).

Left: Baby's dream kitchen is made out of red Vigan brick, old wood, and Romblon marble. Fine Ilocos bricks encompass a cozy oven alcove copied from an old mansion in Vigan, Ilocos. A solid plank of old *narra* wood became the high counter on the kitchen's central island. Three antique doors from Bohol were recycled for the storage room doors.

Below: The old wood table with ball-and-claw feet is a traditional Philippine furnishing. This *mesa altar* is complemented by a *dama juana* (green glass bottle for making vinigar and wine); two wooden accent balls; and a modern ecstatic acrylic painting by designer friend Andy Maluche.

with fine red bricks—"like my friend Marjo Gasser's old kitchen in Vigan!" Antique doors from Bohol now front walk-in cabinets, and a huge slice of polished old *narra* wood is the kitchen counter. Hanging overhead, the large copper pot-rack—bought in a crafts-fair—had been saved for many years, destined for this once and future dream-kitchen.

Outside, in full view against the cemented property wall stands the weathered wooden door of a tribal Ifugao house, mounted with three steps and a small tiled roof—a masterful touch by designer Paras. The Austrias tell their guests it's the doorway to their swimming pool area beyond!

This residence was a first architectural project for designer Eric Paras. His personal style has subsequently evolved from the eclectic into one that embraces modern-minimalist concepts. He declares his designer icons: "Filipinos Lor Calma and Budji Layug for their modernist furniture style; Christian Liaigre for fresh and clean designs fit for tropical countries; Andree Putman for revival of classic-modern furniture; John Pawson for brave minimalism; and Chinese Ming furniture, which can blend well with eclectic and modern interiors."

Left: A spare but colourful bedroom for the Austria's son. Simple Filipiniana furnishing means: a native *papag* (a narrow wooden bed) with an old fashioned *solihiya* (cane-woven) platform; and the traditional wooden *baul* (trunk) at its foot. Note the old rocking chair and the heavy bedside lamp, converted from the molave wood hub of an old sugarcane crusher.

Below: Lumang *baño*—an antique bathroom—as well. Designer Eric Paras creates an eye-catching bathroom with just three old details: a carved wooden archway overhead: an old mountain-cane ladder to add interest and hang towels; plus a old *kamagong* table, which has been reconfigured with a marble counter and a sink.

Above: The master bedroom behind an antique door from Bohol. A neo-classic four-poster bed in wrought iron is surrounded by Philippine antiques: the Tres-Lunas table, a rare three-mirrored marble-topped dresser set; and an oversized *aparador* (wardrobe) from Bohol.

Opposite, clockwise from top left: A small Mexican wall fountain (from House of Precast) has been converted into a front-entrance planter. The entrance arch for visitors incorporates the owner's old windvane and an antique metal bell. The dainty hand is a brass door-knocker, a rare collector's item from Batangas. The glass panelled torch lamp is from Arte Espanol, classic wrought iron suppliers of Manila. This giant water jar with embossed decor is from Indonesia. Paras's terracotta toned wall fountain was inspired by the Mexican *pueblo* designs; the limestone blocks lining the pond are called Piedra Java, quarried in Ilocos.

Right: An old Ifugao granary door has been raised over three steps and sheltered by a tiled awning roof—on the property's perimeter wall. Paras's charming setup provide a visual focus from the *sala*, and "an illusion of something beyond". When asked where the small door goes to, homeowner Gerico Austria quips, "Yes, it leads to our swimming pool compound!" The small Ifugao stool (from RIBA) works as a contemporary side table.

Right: The inner *sala* features a pillow alcove inset in the wall with luxe silk-lined panelling. The gilt framed lithograph above the array of ornate pillows is by maestro Salvador Dali. The ostrich egg lamp (right) is by designer Chito Vijandre. The turned candlesticks are by Marcelo Alonzo of St Nicholas Crafts.

Belle Exotique

If the eclectic style is defined as "selective from varied sources ethnic with modern flair colourful and spirited, exotic artfully unexpected", then this is the most exotic and artful house in this book, the epitome of Filipino house-fashionable and *outré*-eclectic. Homeowners Chito Vijandre and Ricky Toledo have been embroidering their space with imagination for years, designing, redecorating and re-expressing themselves in the house. An effusive spin-off of a European decorative sensibility, the Vijandre house has been called by many names. Today it comprises a proscenium where they collate a dozen Filipino artists' crafts, before the products are sent off for retailing in Firma, their chic boutique in old Malate.

Both home and shop are ultra-stylish settings for exotic accessories. "This space was supposed to be minimal," says Ricky Toledo, "But we find all these beautiful things, and we have to live with them. So—no more minimal!"

The small meeting room where they chat with suppliers is an embroidered Chinoiserie space, called the Asian Room. Here Vijandre's style is displayed in the exotic walls. The room decor started with an antique *obi* or Japanese sash, which was divided to make the delicately padded fabric panels. The surfaces around the window seat are carved to appear like textured, woven leather. Two art-deco chairs, by surface artist Tats Manahan, gleam brightly like cut-out figures.

Below: The Asian Room started with an old Japanese *obi* (sash), cut and pressed onto narrow closet doors. There are three ostrich eggs on Chito Vijandre's tall white lamp; and balletic bird legs under the centre table. Two Chinese inspired lacquered chairs by surface artist Tats Manahan look like modern cut-out figures.

Right: A retro-modern corner features the minimalist leaf-like Ivy seat (seagrass woven over a metal framework) and Shinzhou, the soulful red heart lamp, both creations by Padilla for Locsin International. The haunted figure emerging from the shadows is a signature image by artist Onib Olmedo.

The marbled entrance foyer is a dramatic setting for two unusual chairs created by design-master and modernist architect Lor Calma; both seats combine the finest wicker and sleekest metal legs into minimalist furnishings. Within the inner, neo-classic *sala*, there are two elegant eclectic groupings: a *soigné* pillow-alcove inset in the wall like a decorative French tapestry; and an Empire-campaign *chaise* setting, with the classical grand divan among diverse modern furnishings, each remarkable on its own.

Within this *sala*, Val Padilla has created several unique chairs including the organic leaf-seat Ivy, a sculptural S-chair made of seagrass woven over a metal frame, and the angular armchair Aurora. It is made of pressed bamboo, specially treated to appear like dark wood. He also dreamed up Locsin's funky red heart-shaped paper lamp, Shinzhou. Nearby is a dazzlingly shiny, iron side table by modern artist Gabby Barredo. Interior designer Chito Vijandre's own signatures in the neo-classic room are the outre ostrich egg lamp, a chic low ottoman covered in pale-green ostrich leather, and two miniature Italian greyhounds, Antonio and Tosca.

Left: The lovely chair, Lotus, is designer Betty Cobonpue's graceful signature seat in moulded rattan. Styled upon a barrel in 1969, this sculptural accent is draped like a Japanese *obi*, or a fancy hairdo or a backless gown! Above, the gilded hand of Buddha blesses the Chinese-Filipina furniture designer from Cebu. The walls are given a faux-antique finish by Vijandre's artist friends.

Right: Chito Vijandre's eclectic dining suite looks out to a lush oriental water garden, while it backs up to wrap-around mirrors. The smart black leather and wood dining chairs are original Art-Deco items, saved from an ancestral house. They gather well around the frosted glass table, arrayed beneath an ornate crystal chandelier from Venice, Italy. The centrepiece comprises a gathering of Chinese Tang terracotta figures. The neo-classic embossed and moulded walls are adopted from Pompeii and Egypt.

Left: A fine coconut 'fabric' woven from minuscule coco-beads is draped as a textured shade over an ostrich egg table lamp! Such *bellissima* ideas and exotic accessories are from Firma's new-found supplier, Catalina's of Bacolod.

Below: A wide-angled armchair and artist Gabby Barredo's medieval metallic side table stand out against dazzling perforated walls. The Aurora armchair, designed by Val Padilla, is constructed of pressed bamboo core. The bleached coco-shell throw-pillow is by Catalina's.

Above: Close up of a dainty wall detail from the Vijandre-Toledo private inner sanctum called the Oriental Room. The wooden detail is carved by Pampanga's traditionally ornate furniture makers. The bejewelled tassel comes from Firma, exotic boutique of Malate, Manila.

Left: Eclectic interior design takes its elements from varied periods and cultural references. The Napoleon campaign *chaise* in French stripes—the homeowner's "chair of desire", produced by the neo-classic traditionalists Designs Ligna—sits well amid Chito Vijandre's exotic art-deco window treatments. The low mint-green ottoman is covered with ostrich leather from Davao.

Left: The *sala* is a Filipino fusion scene built around a vibrant painting by National Artist HR Ocampo. The eclectic setting mixes rustic, neo-classic and modern-style furniture with aplomb—a neo-classic armchair (left) by Linea is teamed with a modular hemp-woven sofa by Union Square. Modern fossil stone coffeetable and lamps by stylist and designer Leo Almeria.

Retro Fusion

The Makati home of Victor and Edna Reyes was restyled to become retro-eclectic. The original CC de Castro architecture provided the shell with adobe exteriors, floating ceilings, poured marble floors and a split-level structure. The interior surfaces offered diverse textured backgrounds: layers of old red brick and mixed blue tilework on the *lanai*; pale olive stucco walls and warm parquet flooring, plus a faux-timber white finish on the cement walls of the foyer.

This gracious old space was reinvented by designer Leo Almeria, demonstrating his modern, eclectic flair. He mixed fine and folk art, rustic crafts with sleek, contemporary furniture, and Filipino paintings of the 1960s with indigenous 1990s handicrafts. The result is an adept diverse composition, showing off some of the country's modern classic furniture-makers.

The Almeria 'look' is, as author John Wheatman reflects, a "combination of beautiful and idiosyncratic items. The whole combination is the essence of the design. It is the crowded assemblage of things artfully arranged aimed to give an instant lived-in look. The cluttered stylist makes sure every room has something rare, witty or artistic to hold it together."

The home's shaded *lanai* offers two stylish lounge settings. On the stone bench coloured by Mrs Reyes's variety of blue tiles, Almeria heaps

Above: Retro elegance in the Reyes's home entrance. The foyer walls are treated with faux-wood treatment and whitewash. A glass topped half-moon console table (Yrezabal) bears a romantic milkglass lamp, an Ifugao basket and old ritual box, and a modern resin-art display plate (Johanna's of Bacolod).

Right: A Cleopatra 'period' *chaise* in olive vinyl and wrought iron comes from the stalwart Arte Espanol; it is matched with a thoroughly modern wood-plank floor lamp with black shade from Renditions of Festival Mall, Alabang, Manila. The small wrought iron table is the 'Zulu' design by much-awarded designer Ched Berenguer-Topacio. The glass and wood serving tray on the divan is a modern design by stylist Leo Almeria. The *naïf* style mural of a village amid the jungle is from Pengosekan, Bali, circa 1975.

throwpillows in shaggy cotton-rag and crisp rattan-wicker weave. Then he conjures a *soignée* scene around the Cleopatra divan—a neo-classic *chaise* designed in the 1980s by Roland Laurena for Arte Español, Manila's most versatile wrought iron supplier. The divan is complimented by a wooden plank floor lamp, shaded in black, by Renditions.

Two *sala* settings cleverly mix varied furnishings while keeping the classic Filipino artwork as central focus. These comprise traditional masterworks by Amorsolo, HR Ocampo, and Saprid, and modern arts by Orlina, Veneracion and Garcia. The furniture includes pale new tables by Yrezabal, all country-modern designs combining gracefully moulded, Permacane laminated rattan with giant bamboo, fossil stone or bevelled glass. The *sala* settings combine rustic, hemp-woven sofas (Union Square) with stylish neo-classic armchairs by Linea and handbeaten wrought-iron classic works by Berenguer-Topacio. The minimalist lamps are by Sicangco, and stone and resin accessories by Almeria.

The foyer displays both tribal artefacts and modern handicrafts. Yrezabal's console table with long, sinuous legs works well with the grouping of Filipino Art Nouveau frames of the family. The glass tabletop holds an Ifugao ritual box, an elegant milkglass lamp, and coconut-inlaid plate by Johanna's Craft of Bacolod.

Opposite, clockwise from top left: Two settings by Almeria: The Modern Asian Table features a dramatic red charger painted by Danilo Garcia and black fossil-stone tray by Almeria; Visayan Suite comprises a chic square black plate (Cardinal Ceramics) with a Samar place-mat and coco-shell flatware from Marcelo Alonzo. Two unusual lamps: Sliced stone exudes soft garden light by candle or bulb; from Stone Symphony Corp, Tarlac; arty nature-lamp features a 'viney' base made of coco-twigs; and an acrylic lampshade pressed with fossilized mango leaves; designed by individualist David Villanueva for Ilonggo International, Bacolod.

Above: The roughhewn stone bench displays Edna Reyes's '70s collection of blue tiles. The wicker pillows are designer-creations by S.C. Vizcarra.

Right: The open-air *lanai* comprises diverse focal points for social gatherings. This wood-framed weaving loom, rigged with a canvas hammock, makes for comfort and conversation during the Olbes parties. The wood relief propped under the giant birds' wing plant, "Monk in the Wine Cellar", is carved by homeowner Antonio Olbes.

Native Treasures

"A good home changes and evolves with you—a good home is never done," writes John Wheatman in *Meditations on Design*. "Use natural resources. Home can be a sensual delight, with simple or intriguing arrangements of pods and seeds and spices reminders of earth and Mother Nature, amid luxurious resonance of modern interiors."

A long-cultivated taste for the ethnic artefacts from the Philippine highlands, as well as classic antique furniture of the lowlands, have fuelled Maricris Olbes's instincts for always interesting, always tasteful home decoration. Conceived with imagination and flair, and enlivened with a constantly renewed display of ethnic treasures, the Olbes's home is an exquisite salon that dinner guests mention for months after an invitation.

The open-air *lanai* alone comprises diverse ethnic focal points combined with an artistic sensibility. A singular Ifugao artefact (a high-backed wooden bench carried by three carved warriors) and a wood-framed weaving loom, rigged with a canvas lounging hammock both instill comfort and conversation during parties. Most of Ms Olbes's unusual ethnic treasures such as her three primitive Tausog standing figures, carved wooden spoons and folksy low-seated *bankitos*, were sourced over the years from tribal art dealer, Ricky Baylosis.

The ethnic folk-art pieces are seamlessly integrated with the modern artworks, primarily sculptures by her brother-in-law, Eduardo Olbes, a modern artist based in Mexico. The *lanai's* casual dining table features a black granite tabletop

Above: A stoney installation of rice flour grinders nestles amid the ferns. A giant glass bottle, a *dama juana*, serves as a greenhouse for fresh ferns, allowing for several days of splendid display. The *lanai*'s ethnic quarter is furnished with three Tausog man figures from Mindanao and a large high-backed, black-wood bench carried by three carved Ifugao warriors.

Right: The ethnic folk-art pieces are seamlessly integrated with modern art-works. In the front garden, Eduardo Olbes's two stone house sculptures were inspired by the weathered Tausog gravemarkers on the *lanai*.

Above: The *lanai*'s casual
dining table, by Filipino artist
Eduardo Olbes, includes a
black granite tabletop over a
rough-finished pedestal
and a central Lazy Susan of
burnished molave wood.
The bar comprises a stone top
over a base incorporating
four antique church panels.
The contemporary rattan
chairs are from Borders,
Makati. Artwork on the easel
is by abstract modernist
Fernando Zobel.

Left: A cultivated taste for ethnic artefacts and a love for natural treasures make the Olbes *lanai* an exquisite salon. The rattan wicker furniture is from Mehitabel, Cebu. On the wood slab coffeetable from Lightworks, Manila, are laminated plates and bowls from Negros, displaying seeds, pods and shells. Around the space are giant sprays of dried wildflowers and fresh blooms.

Right: Small wooden *anitos* (carved figures) and the wood saddle atop a fine antique *mesa altar* (table) from Terry Baylosis. On the wall is Maricris Olbes's beloved tropical palm prints by Fr. Blanco.

Below: Small figurines from Ifugao before a black resin display plate with corn husk motifs (Bacolod, Negros). A wooden plow has been converted into a lampstand, by Palayan Lamps. The metal-based table with a rattan woven surface is from Borders, Makati.

over a rough-finished pedestal, with a Lazy Susan server of burnished molave wood sunk right to the table level. In the front garden, Olbes's two stone sculptures were inspired by the weathered, grave-marker sculpted horse on the *lanai*. A giant obsidian tortoise sculpture swims in a wok of pure white sand.

The *lanai* is graced, too, with the country's finest contemporary rattan wicker furniture from Mehitabel's of Cebu and Borders of Makati (specialists in a 'transitions' style ranging between traditional, modern and minimal). But the *lanai's* real cachet is in the organic, natural accents. As an avid crafts-watcher, Ms Olbes has sourced most exotic creations from the provinces—as boxes and plates laminated with coconut shell or corn husks, "Imagine," she exclaims, "Cynthia Flores in Bacolod recycles corn husks and throwaway materials!" On display are huge sprays of fresh flowers, and fresh ferns and heliconias arranged in a giant bell jar, greenhouse-style. A woven presentation tray offers more natural accents of seeds, pods and ostrich eggs. Ms Olbes maintains a garden of earthly, ethnic delights.

Left: A Mediterranean patio dressed in low-slung French windows and warm afternoon light. The sunny blue and yellow ceramic tiles were sourced in southern Spain. In the corner stands an ebony wood sculpture, "Waterfall", by the homeowner's artist-brother Eduardo Olbes.

Below: Native treasures are complemented with natural details. These two tall bamboo candleholders (by Cosonsa, Cebu) are ever ready to light up a gathering. Bright sprays of flowers are arranged weekly, keeping the Olbes house fresh and alive.

Left: Modern organic ideas perform a rustic medley. Fine seagrass rope and sleek metal frames comprise a sophisticated screen and barstool. Natural and industrial materials are fused together by Val Padilla for ManilaPearl Corp. The Ifugao rice container and giant storage basket become ethnic side tables; the large cotton-rag throwpillows go everywhere.

Rustic Medley

The elegant home of Hans-Juergen Springer is a bungalow house of notable architectural design. A large residence designed in the 1950s by architect Alfredo Luz, it comprises a flat concrete roof over a sprawling G-shaped footprint. A glass-walled house, it is a retro-contemporary affair. All rooms have twin sets of sliding-glass and screened panels and are oriented to look into pockets of Japanese-inspired gardens or green yards. Its courtyard gardens are sheltered by perforated curtain walls which allow the passage of light. The interior space is wide, open and flexible, and perfect for expats' entertaining.

The house has a rustic, eclectic interior, replete with fine wood furniture and fields of Oriental wool carpets—mostly geometric and mainly in red. European Hans-Juergen Springer loves Philippine hardwoods in their most refined forms—with exquisite bone-inlay or with simple polished lines often found in old Tagalog houses. The centre of the spacious *sala* is a medley: a rustic whole-bamboo sofa is wrapped in colourful *ikat* blankets while giant cotton-rag floorpillows are casually piled around a long, low wooden *dulang*, a farmer's table. A wide array of native Filipino baskets, usually fishing or farming tools, have been transformed into assorted table lamps. In the evenings, these basket lamps glow within the house while *capiz* globe-lamps, hanging from the trees, shine through the wrap-around glass walls.

From the diverse wood, bamboo and cane-weave collection, stylist Aida Concepcion has conjured several rustic-elegant settings alongside some new

Above: A Bauhaus-inspired setting. The Valentino chair is an eminent ivory leather upholstered armchair; paired with Roxanne, a bleached wood missile-based floor lamp with *capiz*-finished lampshade. Designs by Val Padilla for Padua International.

Right: The precious Philippine shell, the Mother of Pearl, has become the dazzling medium of a modern artwork by German jeweller and artist in residence in Manila, Hans Brumann.

Below: Folk art and modern art blend in the sunlight. The homeowner treasures fine Philippine hardwoods, especially in Bulacan-style furnishings inlaid with bone and dark *kamagong* wood. The mixed-media painting of Filipino playing cards, entitled "Gutom" (Hunger) by modern artist Brenda Fajardo, stands amidst an array of Asian pottery.

eclectic scenes. Fine pieces from the Springers' traditional collection are combined with contemporary fabrics or modern furniture made with sleek, new-tech materials.

Several suppliers contribute modern creations in new materials. Silk Cocoon, the fabric design partnership of Korean Lee Il Yun and Filipina Jean Goulbourn, adds its elegant touch through silk drapes, in turn accented with twigs and twisted vines. Padua International furnishes a modern corner with a handsome ivory-leather armchair, Valentino, together with a missile-shaped, bleached-wood floor lamp, with its unique shade in a *capiz*-like finish. Both items bear modern airs inspired by the functional aesthetic of Bauhaus, as interpreted by designer Val Padilla for Padua. Finally there are the new seagrass-and-metal duets from ManilaPearl: the Viola chairs and sleek screen divider combine twisted seagrass rope with metal tubing. "The design shows a Zen principle in its simple but sophisticated look," explains designer Padilla, "Thus fusing together natural and industrial materials."

Left: The Victoria fibreglass vases. Fanciful fruit and plant vessels are made of raw fibreglass tubing, coconut twigs, and tiny white shells. This Mugna 2001-awarded collection was designed by Christina B. Gaston for Hacienda Crafts, Bacolod.

Opposite: The lifestyle lies in the gracious details.
Clockwise from top left: An afternoon's lemon iced water deserves a dainty shelled net cover from Regalong Pambahay, Ortigas, and an antique water pitcher, courtesy of Nena Borromeo. Outdoor tables with mosaic tiles, from Amazing Space, Shangrila Mall. Ananas fabrics in *piña-seda*: *piña*—the unique thread from wild pineapple plants, is blended with Philippine silk. The Springer *sala* comprises a bamboo sofa, rattan coffeetable, and shades and cushion covers made of fine silk with *abaca* inserts, by Silk Cocoon, Makati. Colourful close-ups of retro-modern resin-mosaic lamps designed by consultant Josef Crisanto for Raphael Legacy Designs of Cebu. Viola dining chairs in seagrass and metal tubing, from Manila Pearl Corp.

Right: Elegant *papag* in the garden. A refined Philippine daybed or divan, displaying rattan cane weave and fine bone inlay, is complemented by a modern bamboo planter and native bamboo fishtrap—now upturned and transformed into a glass-topped table. The colourful throw is a Maranao *malong* from Lanao, Mindanao.

Tropical Accents

Creativity with natural materials remains the Filipinos' forte—they weave, carve, mould, inlay, or laminate, with wood, clay, vines, seeds and grasses. Spurred by increasing competition and fewer resources, Filipino designers are toning down the ethnic souvenir look, and turning to 'soulful creativity' for modern and international designs.

Top row, middle: 'Pinchers' crabshell veneered tables by Corito Yu for Techmasters.
Top row, right: Unica shakers from MZR Industries.
Bottom row, middle: Chalice stoneware dish from Cardinal Ceramics. Resin candy trays by Reena Pena of Silay Crafts.

Delightful Table Settings

Even for traditionally utilitarian tableware, there are endless creative permutations. With distinctively Philippine flair, interior designer Leo Almeria creates unusual table settings from rustic elements such as hand-painted crockery, coco-shell spoons and brown rice grains, and placemats comprising plaitings of *ticog*, *runo* or bamboo. Some of these table settings display hand-painted plate chargers by artist Danilo Garcia. Stylist Almeria also designs accessories of fossil stone, glass and antique-finished resin.

On the other hand, architect Wendy Regalado has styled several settings using the moulded stoneware of Lanelle Abueva, creative potter of Antipolo. Abueva supplies custom crockery to the most chic restaurants in town, and she also produces Pinatubo-ash glazed pottery and a new square dish collection.

As for spoons, there is, beyond common coco-shell spoons, endless ideas derived from bone and horn—of the carabao! Mrs Evelyn Monroy of Aksessoria Designs has built a craftsy business out

Opposite: Mother of Pearl shell giant serving spoon upon a Heart of Mary leaf; courtesy of its Mexican homeowner. A leaf-themed soup bowl and plate from Cardinal Ceramics, styled by Leo Almeria. Blue-hued setting of stoneware plate, coco spoons, and tassled serviette, from Regalong Pambahay, Manila.

Clockwise from top left: Modern flatware comes standing arty and upright, or in animal prints in a display dish, by Celestial Arts, Manila. Artist-potter Ugu Bigyan's country teapot with a tree-branch handle, on a reed tray by Renato Vidal of First Binhi Corp. Imaginative rice paddles created from carabao horn and coco-wood by Aksessoria Designs, Manila.

of recycled carabao materials and imagination—check out her handmade rice paddles!

Plates in contemporary shapes and colours are supplied by Cardinal Ceramics in Makati, while creative flatware hails from Borders, MZR, Marcelo Alonzo and Celestial Arts, Cebu. The latter, Celestial, produces carved wood handles on stainless flatware, designed using amusing animal themes.

The common *capiz* shell of traditional window panes has lately been pressed into new uses—dainty bowls, plates and teacups. Developed by the Chan family of Shell Arts Company, the new *capiz* is dyed in pastel tones, swathed with resin, and served with a pearly touch.

Sometimes table settings thrive on the eclectic mix of elements. For example, designer Chito Vijandre goes modern as he mixes artists and artisans, textures, colours, and cultural references. He sets a tawny animal-horn bowl from India with a napkin of fine Belgian bobin lace, a lacquered lotus tray by surface artist Tats Manahan, and serves on coco-shell placemats by Catalina's of Bacolod.

Clockwise from top left:
A horn and wood composite: notched bamboo flatware from Maharlika Collection by MZR, buffalo horn bowl from India, carabao horn spoons from Aksessoria Designs, on two-toned wood chip placemat by Tess Pasola for Catalina Embroideries. New products of the Shell Art Company, Manila—two settings of pearly new *capiz* tableware: an earth-toned suite of rice bowl and tray, and a mix-n-match of sky blue dishes in laminated *capiz* shell.

Clockwise from left: Rustic breakfast setting styled by Almeria on reed placemat from Leyte; unique cabbage-leaf plates courtesy of Mrs Edna Reyes; forged metal flatware from Borders, Makati; *nito* napkin rings by Marcelo Alonzo of St Nicholas Crafts. Laminate *capiz* bowl by Shell Art Co., Manila, and coco-shell placemat, by Tess Pasola for Catalina Embroideries. A hand-painted plate charger by Danilo Garcia; styled by Leo Almeria; wicker pillow by SGVizcarra c/o Rustan's. Gilded serving tray by artist Tats Manahan for Firma Shop, Malate; lotus plate-charger courtesy of Chito Vijandre; beaded *abaca* chopsticks holder by Tadeco Co., Davao. Rustic teacups on a red leaf, by Ugu Bigyan of Quezon.

Trendy Receptacles

Food vessels can express a homeowner's taste, wit and humour, or a love of natural material and local craftsmanship. The alchemy comes in the creative designs chosen. The raw materials used are humble bamboo, coco-twigs and *capiz* shells, refined and remoulded with clear resins and imagination.

Resin has become a modern Filipino craft. Common organic materials are combined and reshaped, with resin as the binder, into functional forms or structures—especially by modernist designers like Louisa Robinson and Gilles Pochiet of Cebu, both now creating sophisticated biomorphic vessels. These new 'resin arts' are Philippine creations to rival Thailand's lacquerware craft!

Negros Province has become the centre of resin crafts. Home products are made by recycling waste materials into craftsy home ware. The rustic materials of bamboo and coconut are pressed into stylish plates, trays or candleholders, while cracked shells or sliced poles are used as motifs and incorporated within laminated decor items.

Clockwise from top left: Two nesting resin bowls, embedded with coco-shell and bamboo pieces, from suppliers in Bacolod, Negros. Kitchen baskets and wine-carriers made of pandan, the humblest leafy material, framed with tin and ceramic, by Reeds Co., Manila. Decorative trays feature bamboo sliced crosswise into 'bubble' rings, by Johannas of Bacolod; and bamboo flattened and beaten for multi-hued servers, by Rebena Co., Iloilo. Whimsical pompom flower vases made of wood shavings, dyed pastel and pretty by Papuri Crafts, Manila.

Clockwise from top left: Exquisite candy dish made of a Mother of Pearl shell upon three silver fish, by Cosonsa, Cebu. Cubist-modernist accent vase in stainless steel, from Firma Shop, Manila. Red and black laminated serving bowls, inspired by Chinese porcelain spoons; by Gilles Pochiet for Cielito, Cebu. Edgy modern saucer as table accent in welded wire, by Ann Pamintuan of The Gilded Expressions, Davao. Storage baskets for kitchen or bath, by Reeds Co., Manila. Fanciful ashtray accent in silver and coconut shell; by Cosonsa, Cebu.

Designer Furniture

Individualist styles in furniture and furnishing are emerging islandwide as Filipino designers and suppliers are using more ingenious designs and employing new natural materials; creative talent is increasingly recognized in product development. Through concerted efforts such as Movement 8, driven by Eli Pinto Mansor and Budji Layug, design personalities are emerging and uplifting both product high-end quality, and national image.

Today's rising star in furniture design is Kenneth Cobonpue, a young Cebuano designer, who has a unique East-West aestheticism. His modernist sensibility retains a love for indigenous materials and the warm, natural appeal of Asian furniture, thus he wraps rattan splits over steel frameworks in his Yin-Yang cubist chair and voluptuous Pigalle chair.

Dedicated to training and development within the design industry are two women who lead the Designers Guild of Cebu: Debbie Palau and Corito Escario-Yu. Palau, who studied ecology of materials in Germany, creates playful organic furnishings

Opposite, clockwise from top left: The Jessica lounge chair and footstool comprise rawhide and rope woven in a zigzag pattern on a steel frame; design by Fil-Am Jofel Babaran for Arte Cana. An armchair in open weave leather-core strips, by Debbie Palau for Design Ventures, Cebu. Glass-topped dining table with a massive ribbon-shaped base clad in golden rattan weave; by Allan Murillo for Murillo Inc., Cebu. Brightly dyed leather sling chairs and bamboo pole lamps, by Ramon Castellanos of Disegno en Asia, Cebu.

Clockwise from top left: Folkloric aparador (cabinet) with multi-hued matting motif, by Disegno en Asia, Cebu. Rattan Victoria sofa with roll-over arms, by Murillo Inc., Cebu. Three-legged accent table in bleached mahogany wood and burnished metal; by Padua International. Target seat with twine-covered back-rest and shaped metal legs; designed by Corito Escario-Yu for Techmasters Inc., Cebu.

with a wide variety of materials. Escario-Yu, the modernist, works with high-tech shaped metal, moulded stone, volcanic ash, and crabshell finishes. "We've been attracting world attention because of design. Our biggest success is that we have brought ethnic and indigenous materials to a modern, contemporary level that is still distinctly our own."

Also from Cebu is the romantic revolutionary Ramon Castellanos of Disegno en Asia, who approaches design with whim and fantasy, even while he celebrates local materials: "Stylistically his works follow the spirit of neo-vernacularism, which emphasizes the use of traditional, indigenous materials and iconography. His furniture designs comprise an exotic panache of organic indigenous raw materials and a renaissance of fine craftsmanship."

Casting in a similar romantic line but adhering to more conventional grace, Allan Murillo, designer-owner of Murillo Corp., Cebu, produces large Victorian sofas and other curvaceous furniture dressed in woven rattan, evincing strong 'period' appeal for the dominant USA market.

Manila's most successful furniture designer on

Clockwise from top left:
The knotted armchair, Malena, is made of golden Permacane with a half-circle backrest covered with fine matting, by Yrezabal Inc., Manila; the natural twined vase at its foot is designed by Carlo Tanseco for The Store Inc. Minimalist dining chair in compressed bamboo core, by Carlo Cordaro for FilVeneer Cebu. Retro-flavored Ibis side-chair on spindly metal legs, with upholstery of carabao hide woven in a herringbone pattern, designed by Jofel Babaran of Arte Cana Inc., Manila.

Clockwise from top left:
Two trim, silver leafed Jigsaw modernist metal tables by Edgar Guerrero won an Estilo Award in Cebu's 2001 furniture exhibition. Below it, an oversized Grid table comprises polished wood banding over wicker-weave cushion, by Pacific Traders Inc. for Borders, Makati. Two smart designs from Padua: An ultra-chic wedged sofa, Leonardo Seater, and a graceful S-shaped *chaise lounge*, Louise, done in weaves of natural *abaca* fibre. Designs by Val Padilla for Padua International.

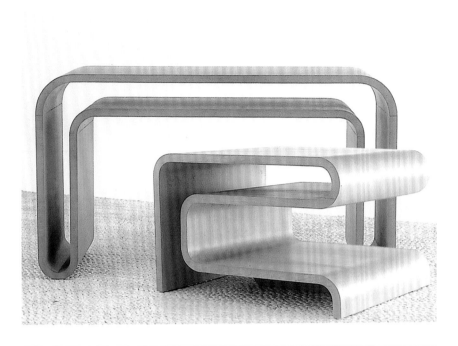

the international scale, Budji Layug, has consistently fashioned fresh designs using indigenous materials, from whole bamboo poles in the late '70s to beaten bamboo, split rattan, and fine-leather weaves today. Budji's works emphasize the fusion of the new and the natural, incorporated within graceful profiles of contemporary furnishings.

Manila-based furniture designer Val Padilla has consulted for over 100 companies in 30 years and created distinct identities for different suppliers, his top clients being major exporter Locsin International and Padua International. Padilla emphasizes that there is a need to create furniture for the high end of the market as it is now impossible to compete against the Asian neighbours' pricess.

Other Filipino modernists include Milo Naval of Evolve Designs—a bold and natural designer famed for bold, modular furnishings in earthy natural materials—and Carlo Cordaro, who pioneered the use of wood veneers in contemporary designer furniture; Cordaro's company, Cebu FilVeneer, has established a thoroughly clean, avant-garde geometry in furnishings.

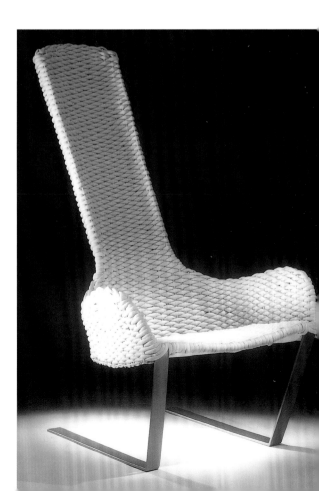

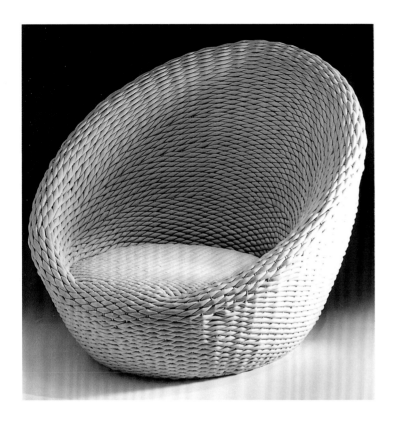

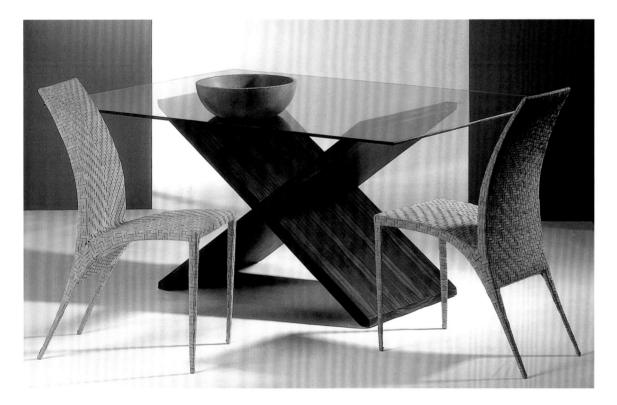

Opposite, clockwise from top left: Sophisticated turn-back two-levelled tables in fine bleached wood veneer, by environmental supplier, Carlo Cordaro for FilVeneer Cebu. Handwoven white kid-leather makes a remarkable textured skin on the Ovo Bird's Chair, by Val Padilla for Padua International. A circular club chair clad with bleached banana trunk, designed by Leo Yao for Diretso Trading Inc.

Clockwise from top left: The original Ovo lounging *chaise* with high-textured white leather weaving; designed by Val Padilla for Padua International. Wood surfacing on S-formed metal-legged chair, by Bernice S. Montenegro for Pacific Traders, Cebu. Modernist dining on the stunning Etnika ebony table with ebony veneered, cross legged base, teamed with woven Gazelle chairs from FilVeneer Cebu.

Maverick designer Leo Yao harbours an avid experimental sensibility with regards new natural materials. First he tries bleached banana trunk; then he weaves rustic upholsteries of different hemps, grasses, and interlocked coconut shells. Yao's latest material is fine bleached raffia from the *buri* palm, woven into a sophisticated armchair designed for the Export Team.

Not least are the pioneers, Philippine furniture's classic senior designers: architect Lor Calma and interior designer Ched Berenguer-Topacio. Berenguer applied her genteel Spanish hand to local furniture, creating contemporary designs in fine leather and hand-beaten wrought iron. Her graceful Petal Collection won the world furniture industry's much coveted Roscoe Award in 1987. The master designer and modernist architect Lor Calma has always nurtured imaginative scale, image play and inventive geometry in his works. His avant-garde chairs (shown on this spread) combine the finest native weaving materials with high-end metal construction to make awesome organic art furnishings.

Clockwise from top left:
A rustic-textured Cube chair is stuffed, segmented and upholstered with native matting, by exporter Beetlejuice Inc. The giant Rocking Chaise is a basketry masterwork in rattan, awarded with the Mugna 2001 for creative originality; design by 20-year-old Cebu Rattan Co.

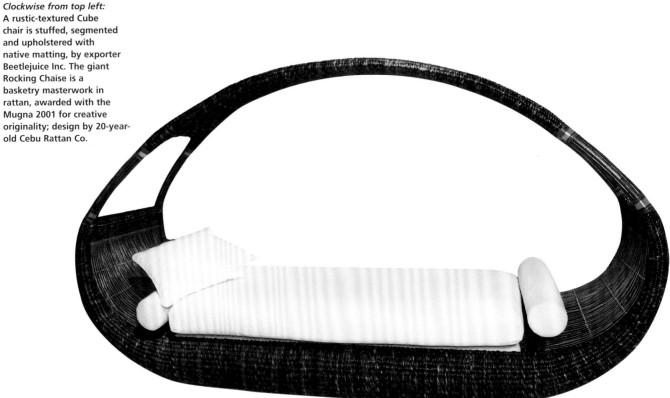

Clockwise from top left:
Leather Grid Armchair is a wide, handsome furnishing standing smart in well tanned leather strips; design by Val Padilla for Padua International. High-tech Bamboo Armchair is a new masterpiece created from bamboo veneer over a solid wood core; by Carlo Cordaro for Cebu FilVeneer. The Hippo is an amazing, anthropomorphic lounging chair—modern architect and designer Lor Calma combines finest natural weaving and an outré profile in this languid seat.

Clockwise from top left:
Four-corner red wrinkly lamps of woven *abaca* cloth light up a row of *abaca*-wrapped bud vases, by Maricris Brias of Tadeco Co., Davao. A natural forest of whole bamboo candlestands to accent a modern setting; from Padua International. The sleek moderne lamps, Millie and Roxanne bear embossed fiberglass shades with *capiz*-like finish; by Val Padilla for Padua International. The curvy and the segmented accent lamps conjured of handmade paper, by Val Padilla for Locsin International.

Creative Lighting

Lamps and lights are opportunities for creativity, and Filipinos duly demonstrate their knack for designing with unusual organic materials, such as handmade paper and twigs; coconut twigs and translucent *capiz* shells; natural stone, hemp, and fossilized leaves pressed onto vinyl.

The F.A.M.E. annual gifts fair showcases such creative lights, such as Padua International's giant standing floor lamps; graphic designer Tony Gonzales's Japanese-style paper lamps; and designer Val Padilla's statuesque lamps with solid wood bases that are bleached or black, crowned by wide translucent shades with an appealing *capiz* finish. Newcomer David Villanueva of Bacolod-based Ilonggo International sets trends with coconut twig lampstands and fossil-leafed shades.

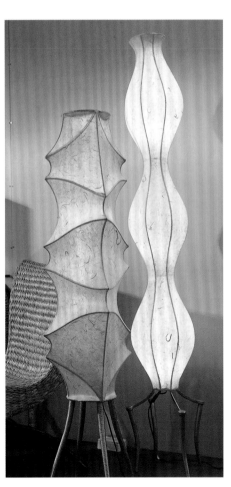

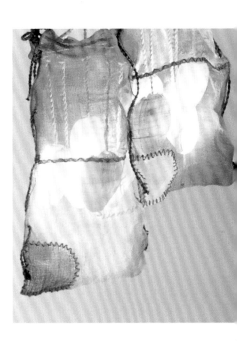

Clockwise from top left:
Translucent *capiz* shell wrapped in layers round a resin vase holds candlelight within, by Tony Gonzales of A Greeting Card Co. Tin leaf-cutouts reflect candlelight in the evening; designed by Ernest Santiago, Laguna. Giant golden shells have light bulbs within and fanciful raffia bags without. Half a dozen paper lanterns, imbued with lines, vines and Japanese airs, by Tony Gonzales of A Greeting Card Co. Textured modular lamps, tables and mirror frames of laminated termite homes; design by Clayton Tugonan for Classical Geometry, Cebu.

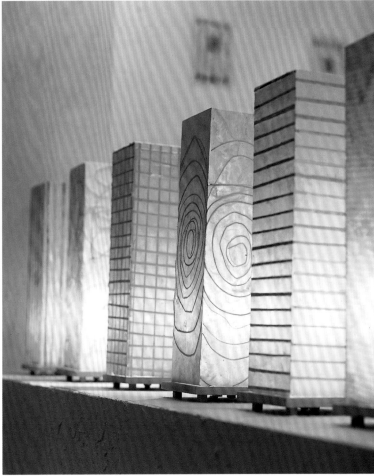

Glorious Fabrics

The fabric of the times is *abaca tnalak*, a rustic cloth handwoven by the T'boli tribespeople of Mindanao. Designer Maricris Brias started a crafts workshop making fine, coconut-beaded *tnalak* items. Six years later Tadeco Co markets soft furnishings in a global way! Mindanao's *abaca* fibre finds another champion in the Astorga Handloom company in Davao. Entrepreneur Priscilla Tiongko turns versatile *abaca* into Roman window shades and throwpillow covers.

When *abaca* is married to rayon and modern colours, one gets drapery bearing unique sheen and body. Fabric designer Elisa Reyes combines banana (*abaca*) fibers with rayon and linen; and harnesses palm leaves and stems. She retails through Soumak the delectable fabrics that only insiders know about!

Silk holds its modern own under the name Silk Cocoon, for designer fabrics combining Philippine silk and linen, and natural twigs and leaves for accent and structure. Silk Cocoon, which began in the '90s, produces the silk blends that make the sophisticated upholsteries used in our pages.

Clockwise from top left:
A macramé tie-back, dangling with Philippine shells and refreshing accent for curtains, courtesy of house-proud Baby Austria. Three glorious *piña-seda* shawls, made from finest pineapple fibre blended with Philippine silk; by Jennifer Baum Lagdameo of Ananas Co. The season's finest innovation comprises dyed coconut shell coins woven together into a beaded 'fabric' for accessories such as throwpillows; by Catalina Embroideries of Cebu.

Far left column, from top: Tri-coloured hand-painted banana fabric, courtesy of Dita Sandico-Ong. Colourful Yakan runner and Zamboanga sarong from Mindanao comprise traditional crafts utilized for modern décor.

Left column and below: A pile of smart soft furnishings in neutral tones of grey, from Astorga Handloom Crafts of Davao. Ethnic-rustic *tnalak abaca* covers are detailed with finest coconut shell beadwork; by Tadeco Co, Davao. *Abaca*-hemp covers are trimmed in bold designs in felt, by MKJ Service Link.

Acknowledgments

SPECIAL THANKS (for cover shoot):
Lizzie Zobel (homeowner); Aida
Concepcion (stylist); Simon
Bagabaldo (assistant); Delfin E.
Peñero (*chaise* designer, Trayline
Inc.); Carlo Tanseco (eggshell vase,
The Store Inc.); Roberto Locsin
(vine lamp, Locsin Int'l); Su
Llamado (Princesa *piña* shawl,
Palawan); Leo Yao (designer,
Export Team Inc.); Felix Guinto,
Eusebio Yu, Boldy Tapales (photog-
raphers); **Project hosts:** Hans
Juergen Springer; Mr & Mrs Carlos
Cruz; Bernadette and Ed Gallego;
Ruby Salutan (Cebu Furniture
Industries Foundation).

FURNITURE
Arte Espanol, #2 Don Bosco St, Makati,
MMla. Tel 02-867-1525
B-at-Home Showroom, 235 Nicanor
Garcia Ave, Bel Air II, Makati , MMla.
Tel 02-896-6316 <budji@mozcom.com>
Berenguer-Topacio Inc., Magallanes
Village, Makati, MMla. Tel 02-852-7746
Borders, 2291 Pasong Tamo Ext
Makati, MMla. Tel 02-813-0112
<borders@info.com.ph>
Budji Collection, 233 Nicanor Garcia Ave
Makati, MMla. Tel 02-890-1152
Cebu FilVeneer, Mactan Economic
Zone, Cebu. Tel 032-340-0301
<www.filveneer.com>
Designs Ligna Inc., #16 First Avenue,
Bagumbayan, Taguig, MMla.
Tel 02-837-2872 <dligna@skyinet.net>
E. Murio Inc., Merville Industrial
Complex, Paranaque, MMla.
Tel 02-776-5491 <bristol@pacific.net.ph>
Evolve Designs Inc., Susana Vill, Quezon
City. Tel 02-932-7679 <evolve@sfi.com.ph>
The Gilded Expressions, Apo View
Hotel, Davao. Tel 082-221-0748
Interior Crafts of the Islands, 3-A
Gen. Maxilom Ave, Cebu City.
Tel 032-233-4045

<kenneth@interiorcrafts.com.ph>
Lightworks Resources, Sunriser Village,
Llano Rd, Caloocan City, MMla.
Tel 02-843-6142 <www.lightworks.com.ph>
Linea Furniture, Almeda Bldg, 1014 Pasay
Road, Makati, MMla. Tel 02-845-3023
Locsin International, Ersan Bldg, #32
Quezon Blvd, Quezon City, MMla.
Tel 02-443-0763 <www.locsin.com.ph>
Lor Calma Design Inc., 186 Salcedo St,
Legaspi Village, Makati, MMla.
Tel 02-817-8465 <lcdinc@skyinet.net>
ManilaPearl Corp., #145 Sumulong
Highway, Antipolo, Rizal.
Tel 02-645-3699 <mnlpearl@csi.com.ph>
Mehitabel Furniture Co Inc., Sanson
Road, Lahug, Cebu City. Tel 032-231-
4039 <jbooth@mehitabel.com.ph>
Osmundo Gallery, Unit 303 la O'
Centre, 1000 Pasay Rd, Makati, MMla.
Tel 02-867-2075
Padua International Corp,1171 Mabini
Street, Ermita, Manila. Tel 02-526-7772
<info@padua-intl.com>
Recuerdos Crafts, Paliparan Road,
Salawag, Dasmarinas, Cavite.
Tel 046-540-3287
Renditions, Festival Mall, Filinvest,
Alabang, Muntilupa, MMla.
Tel 02-850-3780 <delco@pworld.net.ph>
Benji Reyes, 8 Provincial Rd, Beverly Hills
Subdiv Antipolo, Rizal. Tel 02-658-3630
Sason Shop Inc., Brgy Alijis, Bacolod
City, Negros Occ. Tel 034-435-4759
<info@sasonshop.com>
Techmaster Furniture, Opao, Mandaue
City, Cebu. Tel 032-346-0127
Union Square Enterprises, Virra Mall,
3rd Level, Greenhills, San Juan, MMla.
Tel 02-927-4261 <unionsq@i-next.net>
Yrezabal Inc., Platinum 2000 Bldg, #7
Annapolis St, Greenhills, San Juan, MMla.
Tel 02-726-2679

ACCESSORIES
Accessoria, Cabancalan, Mandaue,
Cebu. Tel 032-345-4680
<guilorie@skyinet.net>

Almeria-Castro Inc., 43 Sct. Tuazon St,
Quezon City, Mmla. Tel 02-371-1707
Astorga Handloom Crafts, Bagobo
House Hotel, Gov. Duterte, Davao.
Tel 082-222-4444 <jht@weblinq.com>
Avellana Gallery, 220 Fresno Ave,
Pasay City, Manila. Tel 02-522-9793
<artsaa@evoserve.com>
Cardinal Ceramics, off Kamagong St,
Makati City, MMla. Tel 02-899-3731
Cielito, Dona Rita Village, Banilad, Cebu.
Tel 032-3469389 <circa@cebu.i-next.net>
CSLDI, Lighting Design Inc., Villamonte,
Bacolod, Negros Occ. Tel 034-703-0838
<chrissi@mozcom.com >
Galleria Duemila, 210 Loring St
Pasay City, MMla. Tel 02-831-9990
<duemila@info.com.ph>
Hiraya Gallery, 530 United Nations
Avenue, Ermita, MMla. Tel 02-523-3331
Johanna's, Mt View Subdiv, Mandalagan
Bacolod, Negros. Tel 034-441-0713
<Johanna@bcd.i-next.net>
Papuri Crafts, 2 Jersey St, Project 8,
Quezon City, MMla. Tel 02-929-3319
<papuri@pworld.net.ph>
Raphael Legacy Designs Inc.,
Pagsabungan, Mandaue, Cebu.
Tel 032-345-0241
<raphael@mosaicom.com>
Riviera Clay Inc., 1125 Antipolo Street,
Rizal Village, Makati City, MMla.
Tel 02-896-4930 <rclay@mozom.com>
Silk Cocoon, New World Renaissance
Hotel, Makati Ave, MMla. Tel 02-811-6856
Soumak Collections, 101 Bormaheco
Condominium, Metropolitan Ave, Makati.
Tel 02-890-7784
The Store Co., Inc., 2/F Glorietta 4, Ayala
Center, Makati MMla. Tel 02-438-5522
Tesoro's 1325 A. Mabini St, Ermita,
MMla. Tel 02-524-3936
Ugu Bigyan Pottery, c/o A. Lorayes,
Ayala Alabang, Muntinlupa, MMla. Tel
02-850-9303 <choochoo@i-next.net>

ACCENTS
A Greeting Card Inc., Meliton Espiritu

Cmpd, San Antonio, P'que.
Tel 02-820-9516 <batcave@pacific.net.ph>
Aksesoria Designs, 38 Boston St,
Cubao, Quezon City. Tel 02-416-6266
Amazing Space Inc., ShangriLa Plaza,
Mandaluyong, MMla. Tel 636-0051
Ananas, 102 Esteban St, Legaspi Village,
Makati, MMla. Tel 02-893-4282
Catalina Embroideries, G. Ouano St,
Opau, Mandaue, Cebu.
Tel 032-346-2829 < jls@cnms.net>
Celestial Arts, Blue Ridge,
Quezon City, MMla. Tel 02-647-1110
<pinkcove@hotmail.com>
Cosonsa Manufacturing Inc.,
Mindanao Rattan Cmpd, Alang-Alang,
Mandaue, Cebu. Tel 032-346-5090
Firma Inc., 616 J. Nakpil St, Malate, MMla.
Tel 02-525-5001 <firma@vasia.com>
First Binhi Crafts, 1428 San Andres
Bukid, Sta Ana, Manila. Tel 02-561-7177
<firstbinhi@edsamail.com.ph>
Hacienda Crafts, ANP Showroom, Lacson
St, Bacolod, Negros Occ. Tel 034-435-0716
<hacienda@mozcom.com>
Ilonggo Int'l Home Furnishings, 74-A
Locsin St, Bacolod City, Negros Occ.
Tel 034-434-1196 <ilonggo@bacolod.net>
MZR Industries, 32 Chicago St, Cubao
Quezon City, MMla. Tel 02-724-5450
Reeds, 41 Annapolis St, Greenhills,
San Juan, MMla. Tel 02-723-9378
<reeds@mozcom.com>
Regalong Pambahay, SM Megamall,
Mandaluyong, MMla. Tel 02-638-5478
Rurungan sa Tubod Foundation,
Tel 02-563-2238 <sol@sllamado.com.ph>
Rustan Commercial Corp., Ayala Avenue,
Makati City, MMla. Tel 02-813-3739
Shell Arts Company, Cityland 10/Twr 2,
Valero St., Makati. Tel 02-812-8094
Tadeco Livelihood Centre,
Damosa Building, Lanang, Davao.
Tel 082-235-2135
TN International, Dr. A Santos Ave,
Sucat, P'que, MMla. Tel 02-829-3820
<tnphil@pworld.net.ph>